# IN THE FLOW

*Performance psychology for winning in canoeing and kayaking*

Jonathan Males PhD

Typeset in Meta Serif and Knockout

Editing, design and publishing by UK Book Publishing

UK Book Publishing is a trading name of Consilience Media

www.ukbookpublishing.com

ISBN: 978-1-910223-08-6

Copies are available via *http://performance.sportscene.tv*

*In the flow* is also available as an e-book via online retailers.

Cover photo: Paddler: Mallory Franklin © AEphotos.co.uk / A Edmonds

# Contents

# Acknowledgements

Rob van Bommel of Sportscene encouraged this project from the start and provided great photos. Anthony Edmonds (AE Photos) and Deb Pinniger also generously made their photo libraries available.

I've been fortunate to work with, and learn from, so many great coaches and paddlers over the years, including Jürg Götz, Hugh Mantle, Mike Druce, Peter Eckhardt, Andy Raspin, Geoff Foster, Paul Ratcliffe, Lyn Simpson and Richard Lee.

Bill Endicott deserves a special mention, both for his support and encouragement early in my slalom career, and for reading early drafts of this book and providing very generous and thoughtful feedback.

Thanks to Andrea McQuitty, Luuka Jones, Sabrina Barm and Laura Blakeman who offered such rich insight into women's experience of paddling.

Dr Jo Hudson, Dr John Kerr and Robert Robson ably supported my academic research and helped me to (finally) complete my PhD.

William Winstone, fellow Director at Performance1, helped me test and develop these ideas across different sports.

Finally, thanks to my family who tolerate my time away paddling, and the special times when my beautiful daughters join me on the water.

# Why the fundamentals count

*In 1992 I was coaching the Australian slalom team at the Barcelona Olympics. After a twenty-year gap, slalom was back on the Olympic programme. We spent hours preparing on the new artificial course at La Seu d'Urgell, learning every wave and feature. No one knew what the actual layout of the course would be, but we knew it would be difficult. It was the Olympics after all...*

*We were wrong. TV schedules needed to keep things moving, so the day before the competition we saw a fast, open and straightforward course which skirted the difficult features we'd spent so long practising on. You could almost hear the collective groan of disbelief.*

*Despite their initial disappointment at such a simple course, I watched in amazement as some of the world's best athletes blew their Olympic chances. Despite the simplicity of the gate sequences, many athletes failed to deliver, wilting under the gaze of the spectators, the knowledge that they were being watched by millions of television viewers, and their desperate desire to achieve Olympic success. It worked in our favour: the under-rated Danielle Woodward performed to the level of her ability and won the silver medal for Australia. It was a powerful illustration of the importance of delivering the fundamentals – both technical and psychological – when it counted.*

# Introduction

I've been hooked on kayaking since the age of 12, when I discovered the magical feeling of being able to paddle my own boat and the joys of moving water. It gave me a sense of freedom and competence that I couldn't find on the football field or cricket pitch, and growing up in Tasmania it was important, especially for a boy, to be good at a sport. In my early days I could just as easily be found playing canoe-polo, down-river racing, sea kayaking or river-running. In the late 70s and early 80s Tasmania still had remote and unknown rivers, and I was lucky enough to share in the adventure of first descents. As a teenager, slalom emerged as my priority. For nearly ten years I followed my ambition as a slalom racer, achieving success at a national level and competing internationally on the Australian team at four world championships through the 1980s. Travelling and competing on the slalom circuit was a fantastic, and at times highly challenging experience, that sparked my curiosity about performance psychology and has shaped my life and career ever since. Following my first slalom career, I coached the Australian slalom team at the Barcelona Olympics, then I moved to Britain where I worked as a coach and sport psychologist with talented paddlers and coaches on the British slalom and sprint teams over three Olympic cycles. For the last ten years I've been an active paddler again, running rivers, trying to master freestyle moves, racing slalom and introducing my daughters to the sport.

I completed my psychology PhD in 2013[1], in an attempt to answer the questions I've been asking all these years: What's the connection between what paddlers think and feel and how they perform? How does mental preparation help performance? What do paddlers and their coaches need to do, to ensure paddlers perform at their best when it counts?

This book takes what I've learned over the years and presents it in a practical, accessible format for paddlers and coaches. The material is relevant for competitors in all disciplines as well as for recreational paddlers. I use the terms paddle-sports, canoeing and kayaking interchangeably, so please don't take offence if you feel I'm ignoring your specific craft!

**Section 1** begins by understanding self-confidence, the single most important factor for success and enjoyment in paddle-sports, as it is in most fields of human endeavour. I describe how self-confidence flows from the four *Psychological Fundamentals* of Mastery Motivation, Decision Making, Execution and Teamwork. They are called fundamentals in the same way that edge control, balance, rotation and timing are essential physical aspects of paddling. Understanding and developing the Fundamentals makes the connection between what happens inside your head and how you perform. The psychological Fundamentals develop naturally with experience but I provide specific skills and exercises that you and your coach or sport psychologist can use to increase your capability and speed up your learning in each area.

**Section 2** has six chapters that each address a theme and show how the psychological Fundamentals help performance. Feel free to dip into the chapters that interest you most.

There's a chapter on **competition** that's relevant for slalom, extreme racing, sprint, marathon, ocean racing and freestyle, with real examples from top paddlers and coaches. This will help you develop your own personalised Performance Demand Model and a race day plan to guide you successfully through your event.

The next chapter explores **whitewater paddling** and shows how the psychological fundamentals are just as relevant when you're sitting at the top of a waterfall as when you are on a start-line. I look at risk and decision-making in remote environments, and how to maintain or rebuild confidence after a bad experience.

Chapter 8 tackles **women in paddling**. I was asked to write this by a young man I met paddling with his girlfriend. He was puzzled and frustrated by his girlfriend's behaviour on the river, so I've interviewed some outstanding women paddlers to get their advice and also reviewed the research on the psychological differences between men and women.

Chapter 9, **Paddling with young people**, will be especially relevant if you're a parent or coach. I explain how young people's thinking, feeling and motivation can change through their teenage years and into young adulthood, and what you can do to help them stay engaged and positive.

Next, I look at **canoeing over a lifetime** and the psychological transitions at different stages of life. I show that some real gifts emerge with maturity that mean you can get as much, or more, satisfaction from paddle-sports as the youngsters.

Finally, Chapter 11 closes with some reflections about what **paddling in the natural environment** and in the wilderness has to offer for your mental and spiritual health.

I've provided footnotes for each chapter, but as this is intended to be a practical rather than an academic book, they are meant to help you learn more and feel reassured that I'm not making things up, rather than forming an exhaustive reference list.

*Jonathan Males PhD*

I write regularly on my blog, Diary of a middle aged kayaker, *http://paddleblogs.com/mally/* and I also provide performance psychology resources at *www.sportscene.tv*

If you'd like to buy multiple copies of this book or have any special requests, you can do so at *http://performance.sportscene.tv*

*In the flow* is also available as an e-book via online retailers.

And if you're interested in applying these ideas to the world of business, where they are called the ART of Performance, visit my company website *www.performance-1.co.uk*

# SECTION I

## Self Confidence and The Fundamentals

Self-confidence is the single most important psychological factor in successful sports performance. Self-confidence is based on how you think about a situation and assess your chances of success. It's the realistic knowledge and belief that you are capable of achieving what you set out to do. Self-confidence is more than bravado or naïve optimism – although it's easily confused with both. Truly self-confident paddlers don't need to talk themselves up or talk their competitors down. Truly self-confident paddlers know how to weigh up the risks, and understand that some rapids are better left alone. They also understand that no matter how confident they are in their own ability, that other competitors or the force of a river or ocean remain outside their control, so race results or safety are never guaranteed. Being self-confident doesn't mean you never feel anxious or scared, but it does mean you can deal with these feelings productively rather than them hampering your performance. While some paddlers seem to possess natural self-confidence, the reality is that everyone's self-confidence fluctuates – whether you're an Olympic champion or a raw beginner. So it's important to understand where self-confidence comes from and how you can develop it.

Through my research and over twenty-five years' practical experience with top class competitors and coaches in a wide range of sports, I've identified the four core psychological capabilities that any paddler needs in order to be self-confident and perform competently. By perform, I don't just mean in competition. These same psychological factors underpin your confidence just as much in helping you get down a stretch of Grade 5 as they do when you're sitting on the start line of a slalom or about to hit your entry move in a freestyle event.

Self-confidence comes when you have the right attitude and goals, know that you have planned and prepared well, you know how to focus under pressure and you trust the people around you. I call each of these factors the *Psychological Fundamentals* and each has an important role to play by itself and as one of the foundations of self-confidence.

## The Fundamentals that underpin Self-Confidence

Although we'll be exploring these in greater detail later in the book, here is a brief explanation of these terms and their significance for canoeing and kayaking:

### Mastery Motivation

This is your attitude, determination and commitment to achieve *mastery* over yourself, your competitors and your environment. If you're a competitive paddler, Mastery Motivation underpins your fierce will to win. For a recreational paddler, Mastery Motivation provides the drive to challenge yourself and find the limits of your ability.

**Decision Making**

This is the ability to plan ahead, think clearly and to learn from experience. Making good decisions in your choice of moves in a freestyle event is important, but so too is whether you choose to run a tough rapid or not.

**Execution**

This is the ability to remain totally focused so you can perform under pressure. Executing your skills automatically will help you win a slalom race, and it will also save your life when you need to avoid a hidden log midway down a rapid.

**Teamwork**

This allows you to build effective relationships and get the support you need from coaches, team-mates or paddling buddies. Having a good relationship with your coach, for example, helps sustain your competitive career, and getting on well with your mates on a multi-day self support sea kayaking expedition is pretty useful too.

Think of these four factors as being the psychological equivalent of the physical and technical fundamentals that you need to paddle, like balance, strength or co-ordination. For example, whatever paddling discipline you engage in, you need to balance in your boat. Clearly different disciplines make different demands on your balance; arguably it's really important when paddling a sprint K1 and less critical when playing on a sit on top kayak at the beach. Likewise the psychological fundamentals show up in different ways in different competitive disciplines and paddling environments.

We each have a natural capacity for balance and innate strength, and you can improve your physical and technical fundamentals over time through natural experience or by specific training. In the same way, paddlers have different starting points for each of the psychological Fundamentals because their life experience and personalities are different too. This is the reason that different paddlers vary in their appetite to compete or take risks. Despite these natural differences and whatever your starting point, you can develop all the psychological Fundamentals. By learning about them you will understand the connection between your thoughts and feelings and how you perform on the water. This will help you get more out of your paddling, whatever your paddle-sport disciplines.

Although they are described separately, the Fundamentals work together to support your ability to paddle confidently, and developing competence in one area will have a positive knock-on in other areas. The quality of your Decision Making influences your ability to Execute well, especially when these two components are powered by Mastery Motivation. When good Teamwork is in place too, all four Fundamentals come together to create self-confidence.

The Fundamentals are all underpinned by Reversal Theory[2], a comprehensive psychological model of emotion, motivation and personality. I want to keep the academic theory well in the background, so think of this as being like the operating system on your computer. It's good to know it's there but you don't need to understand every detail about how it works in order to use your computer. Same here – you can develop your self-confidence and each of the Fundamentals without an in-depth understanding of Reversal Theory. For those who want to know more about the theory, follow the footnotes. For everyone else, the basic assumptions of Reversal Theory are that people's motivations and emotion are inherently inconsistent, but that there is a pattern to this inconsistency. Changes, or reversals, in our motivation shape our experience and emotions. So, rather than defining personality in terms of fixed characteristics (traits), Reversal Theory suggests that healthy functioning requires us to be flexible and adaptable. For

AEphotos.co.uk / A Edmonds

example, at times, it's appropriate to be serious and focused, and at other times to be spontaneous and playful. When our state of mind matches the needs of the environment all is likely to be well; when it doesn't we're likely to feel some form of stress. Reversal Theory emphasizes the importance of understanding how a person is experiencing a situation rather than assuming that everyone doing the same activity will feel and think the same way. I like Reversal Theory and have used it extensively in my research and applied work, but I will also point to some other psychological models where they add insight.

Let's look at each Fundamental in turn, and I will help you understand what it is and how it helps performance, the warning signs that suggest you need to work on it, and some practical things you and your coach (if you have one) can do to improve.

---

1. A reversal theory of sport performance, PhD Thesis, Department of Sport Science, Aberystwyth University

2. Two good introductory books are Motivational styles in everyday life: A guide to reversal theory: American Psychological Association. Edited by Michael Apter, 2001; John Kerr's Counselling athletes: Applying reversal theory. Published in London by Routledge, 2001. For an online resource see *http://www.reversaltheory.net/org/*

3. Fast and Clean, DVD, Russ Nichols Production, 1979

# Chapter I
## Mastery Motivation

*"I never quit, I just never quit."*

**– Jon Lugbill, 5 times C1 slalom world champion**[3]

*"Talent is nothing without hard work. It only gives you an advantage in the first steps, after learning the basics. It's hard work that makes the difference."*

**– René Poulsen, medal winning sprint kayaker**[4]

There are many, many, reasons for participating in paddle-sport, and the reasons can change over time, even within the course of an afternoon's river trip. Most people paddle because they find it fun and sociable and they enjoy contact with the natural environment, yet at times canoeing can be terrifying, exhilarating, exhausting and even boring. Not everyone is drawn to competition, but those who do compete have many motivations: some love winning, others hate losing; some want to prove that they are worthy of respect; and some compete just because they enjoy the challenge.

Psychologists have all sorts of theories to describe these different types of motivation and their impact on performance. The truth is, competitive paddlers can and do perform well with all sorts of motivation, and recreational paddlers can enjoy the sport for many different reasons, too. But to increase your chances of staying engaged in the sport *longer* and competing more *successfully,* you need to develop a particular type of motivation called Mastery Motivation.

Mastery Motivation is the desire to be in control of your performance, to perform to the very best of your ability, and to continually challenge yourself. Paddlers with strong Mastery Motivation are highly committed, tough and determined. They are largely self-focused, which means that their ultimate measure is not against opponents but against their own standards. They have a strong desire to win – but only because race results are further evidence that they have performed as well as possible on the day. The real pleasure of winning comes not from beating someone else but from achieving all that they are capable of in that particular moment of competition. Outside of competition it shows up as a desire to test yourself to your *own* limits, whether that's surfing a big ocean wave, venturing onto moving water, or staying upright in a sprint boat for the first time. Paddlers with strong Mastery Motivation are fascinated, even obsessed by their sport. They love studying its history, its intricacies and are always seeking to test the limits.

**A real life example: "I need to know I can race well, no matter how I feel"**

In May 1993, I was coaching the British slalom team and met up with Richard Fox on a cold, windswept Nottingham riverbank. There were two Premier Division races taking place on the weekend. I asked him why he'd come back from training in the sunny south of France, especially for a domestic race like this.

"I've been training really hard and I'm exhausted," Richard told me. "I've got a cold. This will be a tough race and I don't feel like doing it. It's a real hassle to come back, and – as I expected – the weather's bad. But I need to know I can race well, no matter how I feel." He won both of the weekend's races and also his fifth individual World Championship later that year.

# Attributes of Mastery Motivation

Paddlers with Mastery Motivation demonstrate the following attributes:

**They are goal-oriented**

They paddle with purpose and are constantly seeking new challenges. Whether it's the next race or the next waterfall, working towards new goals energizes them. Their goals tend be based on meeting and exceeding their own, rather than other people's standards. Motivation that is based solely on meeting other people's expectations or just on achieving results is often short-lived. Once the result is achieved, then what? Sure, it's possible to re-set goals, but some paddlers report a feeling of deep anticlimax and even depression if their sole focus has been on a single result – even if it's winning an Olympic medal. Mastery Motivation is primarily self-referenced, so as slalom coach Bill Endicott once said, it's about the search for the ultimate run. This attitude makes it easier to stay focused at big events, when there is a risk of becoming distracted by other people's expectations and the lure of 'fame and glory' following a good result.

*"Sport involves sacrifices, but everyone makes their own choices in life and decides which goals to pursue. The important thing is to know what you are doing and why. The results can be achieved with perseverance, commitment, and even a bit of luck."*[5]

Daniele Molmenti, twice K1 slalom World Champion and Olympic Gold Medallist

**They have a strong will to win**

Paddlers with strong Mastery Motivation look forward positively to competition rather than with any sense of fear, because they see it primarily as a chance to test themselves against their own standards. They downplay how they compare to others because they know that they can't control how well other people perform, but they will be fierce competitors, willing to fight hard and never, ever quitting. On a river or sea kayaking trip they will stay positive and committed even when the going gets tough.

**They are self-disciplined**

They do whatever is necessary to prepare and race well, with a positive and professional attitude. This requires high levels of personal maturity and self-discipline. In order for paddlers to *sustain* their Mastery Motivation, they have learned when to rest, recover and look after themselves to guard against injury or burn out. They are adaptable, and can 'buckle down' to complete a hard training session, and also appreciate the times when it's OK to be playful and enjoy messing around on the river.

*"Racing is something that I train for, but more importantly paddling and having fun each day is what I live for."*[6]

Vavra Hradilek, K1 slalom World Champion and Olympic silver medallist

**They have emotional self control**

Fundamentally optimistic, they have learned how to maintain their confidence in the face of risk and uncertainty. Even when they feel nervous, they don't let their worries get the better of them. Paddlers with strong Mastery Motivation feel confident because of quality training, the experience of watching other great paddlers, the support of a coach, friends and family, and through their own self-belief.

**They take personal responsibility**

When things go wrong, paddlers with strong Mastery Motivation will always first look 'in the mirror' to discover what they could have done differently or how they could have prepared better. Only then do they look 'out the window' to see what other people could have or should have done, or take other external circumstances into account. By taking responsibility like this they learn faster and avoid making the same mistakes over and over again.

# Warning signs

There are a number of signs that suggest a paddler needs to work on developing their Mastery Motivation. When do you notice any of these behaviours?

**Paddlers**

- Suffer high pre-race anxiety that prevents them from performing well. This suggests too much worry about the outcome of the event and comparing themselves against other competitors, or worry about living up to other people's expectations;

- Lack confidence in training sessions, and will even avoid competitive training and competition itself. Instead of seeing it as an opportunity to express their ability, competition is viewed as a threat to self-esteem;

- Give up and fail to complete training efforts after making a mistake. Being overly perfectionist gets in the way of learning and performing under pressure. It's important to learn how to 'hang in there' regardless. There are also times in training when making a mistake is a sign of learning and pushing the boundaries;

- Appear to be more concerned about being liked by others or staying comfortable so won't push themselves or others hard in training. This is often the case for teenagers who have a strong need to fit in with their peers;

- Don't prioritise training and preparation, and scatter energy across too many competing interests. Real competitive mastery requires focus and, at the highest levels, obsessiveness;

- Tend to blame other people, their coach, the weather or equipment for a poor performance, and are reluctant to be honest with themselves or listen to objective feedback.

## Summary – Mastery Motivation

Mastery Motivation is the key to your long-term success. By developing it you can sustain your racing career and get more enjoyment from the sport. It's about finding the right mix of goals to move you forward, and developing the personal discipline to train hard and compete fearlessly. If you're not a competitive paddler, it's the drive that keeps you testing your limits and searching for new challenges.

*"What keeps me motivated to train and race? The other guys in the training group, having fun training with your friends. The other motivation has been the desire to be the best. First I wanted to be best in my club, then Norway and then the World. For whom or*

*for what are you ready to train wholeheartedly every day? For myself and my own desires. If kayaking is becoming a job and you do it for the money I think you will not train as well as you need to do to be a winner."*

**Eirik Verås Larsen, Gold Medallist K1 1000m 2012 Olympics[7]**

### Your learning

*AEphotos.co.uk / A Edmonds*

Think of paddlers you know or athletes from other sports who really demonstrate Mastery Motivation. What can you learn from their example?

Reflect on your own career so far, and see if you can identify some examples of when **you** demonstrated outstanding Mastery Motivation. Remind yourself of these examples when you're in the middle of a tough training session.

What is the one thing you can do in the next week to develop, increase or reinforce your Mastery Motivation?

4.  http://www.sportscene.tv/flatwater/canoe-sprint/news/a-great-dane-rene-poulsens-rio-dream

5.  http://www.sportscene.tv/whitewater/canoe-slalom/news/daniele-molmentis-tips-for-the-top

6.  Vavra read an early copy of this book, prompting this great quote

7.  http://www.sportscene.tv/flatwater/canoe-sprint/news/interview-with-multiple-olympic-champion-eirik-veras-larsen

8.  *http://www.sportscene.tv/flatwater/marathon/news/do-the-work-then-go-home-and-dream-interview.*-with-u23-marathon-world-champ

# Chapter 2
## Decision Making

*"My coaches make sure I have the knowledge to do most of the work by myself, they give me pointers on what I should do with my technique and monthly plans year round. This gives me room to make my own plans, and I love it. This gives me a feeling of owning and controlling my progress. It is really motivating and I often do my best sessions after a long day of planning, but of course my coaches look over my plan before I paddle."*

**Morten Minde, U23 K1 World marathon champion**[8]

Decision Making is your ability to think straight, to make good choices and learn from your experience. Making the right decisions can matter a lot, whether it's choosing the fastest lines down a slalom course, working out your tactics for a sprint race or choosing whether you run a rapid or walk around it. It can make the difference not just between winning and losing, but also between getting to the end of a river intact and dying.

Decision Making is best achieved in a calm, rational and disciplined state of mind. Under stress or when tired or rushed, your attention narrows and you can easily miss important information about your environment, or make irrational choices. This is one of the reasons that otherwise smart, well-intentioned paddlers can make disastrous decisions. Effective Decision Making requires a ruthless level of attention to detail, especially when long-term planning for an expedition or mapping out your approach to a competitive season. Self-confidence in Decision Making comes from having successfully dealt with the same challenges in training and knowing that you have the necessary skill, strength and fitness to carry out all the options.

Developing your Decision Making will help you to feel confident and well equipped to make the correct tactical choices and manage risk appropriately. You'll race better and enjoy yourself more on the river.

*AEphotos.co.uk / A Edmonds*

## A real life example: winning Double Gold

Winning one World Championship is special – winning in two different classes in the same year is extraordinary. Yet Dave Florence achieved this in 2013, winning the slalom C1 title and then slalom C2 with team-mate Richard Hounslow. Richard also competed in men's K1. Coach Mark Delaney described how planning and decision making was absolutely central to their success, both in the months of preparation and also at the event itself. In order to deal with the demands of two paddlers competing in three classes, Mark needed to be highly organised and disciplined. He also guided his paddlers to make some important decisions about how they managed the event. They chose to take only one qualifying run before the finals, rather than the two allowed, preserving their energy. Faced with a highly technical and challenging course, they weighed up the level of risk and decided on a conservative plan they were absolutely confident they could deliver, even it was slower than a direct route on several sections of the gates:

> *"The plan is what we executed, we ended up doing four spins, there were maybe some faster options but we decided to err on the side of caution, and at the end of the day it paid off for us."*

**Richard Hounslow, 2013 World Champion Slalom C2[9]**

# Attributes of good Decision Making

Paddlers with well-developed Decision Making demonstrate these five attributes:

**They assess the situation and plan ahead**

They have learned how to plan ahead in great detail and think about the challenges they will face. At a high level, this shows as a determination to 'leave no stone unturned' when it comes to long term planning to achieve their goals, and a real fascination with their sport. In a competitive environment, this starts at a broad level of gathering information about the venue, planning travel and accommodation and thinking about the race schedule. As the event gets closer, this moves to walking the course and thinking about race tactics. Poor Decision Making can lead to problems with Execution when there is uncertainty; however it's important not to get locked into a plan. The very best paddlers are flexible and can stay open to late information to adapt their race plan accordingly.

Here's a great example of how this happens, recorded by David Hughes, describing how freestyle champion Eric Jackson prepared his competition strategy for the 2011 Teva Games. As well as Decision Making, this also illustrates EJ's Mastery Motivation and fascination for his event:

*"EJ scored competitors' rides aloud, "It wasn't 45 degrees." EJ looks at me and explains, "I'm trying to get an ideal of what they're (the judges) counting. It's ICF rules. You only have to be within 20 degrees so it's not that hard to get the moves." Studying the judges and scribes to see if they write after a competitor goes for a move. If the scribe writes then that means the competitor scored.*

*What info is EJ assessing?*

*The athlete wants to know if the judges are easy or tough on giving points. He can gather a different set of info from competitor rides. If the judges are scoring moves easy then EJ will speed his ride and go for more moves equalling a higher score. But if the judges are tough then he'll slow down and focus on hitting the ride with exact planning to have more moves count. He's calculating whether he needs quality or quantity to win based on the character of the judges. As the 5-time world champ he's the master of scoring freestyle and knows the game better than anyone. It's a subtle piece of information that has helped him to dozens if not hundreds of championship titles."[10]*

## They manage risk to get the best possible outcome

Great paddlers know how to manage risk well, and have learned when it is best to play it safe and when it's right to take a more challenging line. They make their decisions on the basis of achieving the best possible outcome, rather than being tempted to take or avoid risks on the basis of fearing that they will appear weak. In whitewater competition there are often choices between 'slower and safer' and 'faster and riskier'. Taking too little risk can be as damaging as taking too much. On a river it's less about speed, and often it's 'less risk means less excitement' or 'more risk means more excitement'. But the consequence of getting the risk level right on a whitewater river or in a remote coastal environment is far more serious than in a race!

*"My team and I have spent years researching waterfalls, honing in our skills and developing experience necessary for running something like Palouse successfully. It was not a mindless huck off a waterfall and hope you live type of thing, it was a calculated decision. The descent would not have worked out like it did otherwise".*

**Tyler Brandt, on running 56m high Palouse Falls.**[11]

**They have great self-awareness**

We might like to think that humans are smart and rational, but the reality is that we make many choices based on too quickly identifying patterns shaped by emotion instead of objectivity. It's hard to take the emotion out of decision making, because our brains are wired to keep it in. Indeed people with certain types of brain damage that interrupt the flow between the emotional and rational parts of their brain are unable to commit to even simple choices. The best we can do is to develop self-awareness so that we can monitor the influence of emotions and our physical state on how we're thinking. So paddlers who can monitor their level of fatigue, stress or anxiety are more likely to take the time to make wiser choices. This is especially important in extreme environments like rivers or the sea, where the consequences of things going wrong are more serious. For example, on a long river trip there may be unspoken pressure to keep moving and get to the finish. This can start to bias a paddler's decisions and lead them to take on rapids that might otherwise be portaged. Self-awareness helps a paddler recognise this pattern, flag it as an issue and negotiate a more measured approach within the group. This makes it possible to keep the whole group moving downstream safely rather than recklessly.

### They mentally rehearse their options

The most experienced paddlers in every discipline have learned how to use *mental rehearsal* to help good Decision Making. They can accurately *imagine* themselves taking different lines down a rapid, or throwing a freestyle combination on a hole, or paddling a gate sequence using different stroke combinations, to help make a decision about what they need to do when they are on the water. This enables them to test their level of confidence and manage risk so they can approach an event in a measured way that builds a great performance, rather than with reckless desperation. Clearly this relies on an accurate self-awareness of technical and physical strengths, which is where a coach's input is vital.

### They learn from their experience

Paddlers who have honed their Decision Making will have learned *how* to learn. This means they are honest with themselves, take accountability for their performances regardless of the outcome and remain open to feedback. So, after a race they will systematically review their performance and take forward the lessons learned to their next event. Here's an example of a paddler learning from experience, from extreme kayaker Rory Woods after poor Decision Making led to a bad swim on the Cauldron Snout, a Grade 5 + fall on the River Tees:

*"I don't think I'm a particularly safe paddler. I really like running stuff blind (or I should say on-sight really), again trusting my judgment to*

*say something is safe based on limited information. This is definitely a bad habit. I get carried away, having fun when I'm paddling well and do silly stuff, and always thought this would be the cause of an accident if anything ever happened to me – not a rapid I had properly looked at from every angle and calmly decided I could do."*[12]

# Warning signs

There are a number of signs that suggest that a paddler needs to work on developing Decision Making. When have you experienced any of these?

**The paddler**

- Often makes poor or rushed tactical choices, for example going out too fast at the start of a sprint race, trying an untested freestyle move in a big competition, or not allowing enough time to walk the course before a slalom race. These suggest the paddler hasn't developed, or isn't implementing, a robust race plan. On rivers, a paddler with poor Decision Making runs unknown rapids without proper scouting or ensuring there is safety cover in place;

- Repeats patterns of errors from one event to another, for example consistently struggling with offset gate combinations over a whole slalom season. This suggests the paddler isn't learning from experience;

- Mismanages risk, either by taking unnecessary risks or by not being bold enough. In slalom, repeated 50-second penalties for necking gates (failing to get the whole head and shoulder within the gate line) might be a sign that the risk equation needs attention. On the other side of the coin, a marathon paddler who doesn't seize the opportunity to overtake a competitor during a slippery portage might need to learn to risk a little more.

*Sportscene / R van Bommel*

# Summary – Decision Making

Decision Making can help you win races by making sure you have planned ahead, considered your options and taken on the right level of risk. It's even more important on a river or in the wilderness – effective Decision Making can help keep you safe and alive.

**Your learning**

Think of paddlers you know or athletes from other sports who consistently make effective decisions. What can you learn from their example?

Think about a time you made a bad decision. What information did you rely on? What information did you miss? What assumptions did you make? How were you feeling, physically and emotionally, before you made the decision? Who else, if anyone, did you talk to?

Now think about a good decision you made and ask yourself the same questions.

What do you notice about the two situations? What can you take forward and apply next time?

*Deb Pinniger*

---

9.   http://www.youtube.com/watch?v=JrLgCTXoxQ4

10.  http://cksblog.com/2011/06/teva-mountain-games-ej-and-dane-discuss-competition-as-they-compete/

11.  http://playak.com/article.php?id=1414

12.  http://playak.com/news.php?idd=2778895668005

# Chapter 3
## Execution

*"I just said to myself there are 18 slalom gates, there's whitewater, I've got my paddle in my hand, I'm sitting in my boat and that's it, no different, keep it simple."*

**Jess Fox, 2012 Olympic slalom women's K1 silver medallist, on what she was thinking about on the start of the 2012 Olympic slalom course**[13]

Execution is the mindset that allows you to be 'in the moment', totally focused on the task at hand, able to ignore distractions and make fast, instinctive responses under pressure. With this state of mind your finely-honed skills and tactics are delivered automatically with minimal or no conscious thinking. It can even include a feeling of effortless performance and of time slowing down. This is often called a state of 'flow', that occurs when you have the necessary level of skill to manage a challenging situation. [14]

There's an important non-psychological point to make about skill acquisition. It takes years of repetitive, high quality training to acquire robust automatic skills. It's important to realise that this comes in two phases, and you can't rush from one to the other. First, just to learn the proper technique, you repeat it in non-stressful situations. But then later you have to stabilize it under pressure, and that's when you want to have more competitive workouts and a lot of race experience. If you start the stressful phase too soon, you risk a deterioration of technique as you revert back to bad habits in a frenzy to keep up. In most competitive disciplines this cycle is repeated every year, so there is a phase of 'off-season' training when the focus is on revisiting and enhancing basic skills before moving to the competitive season when the focus is on delivery under pressure.

You need to be able to access your Execution mindset when the time comes to race or perform under pressure. Paddling a slalom course at race pace, navigating a difficult stretch of whitewater, or completing a complex freestyle sequence can't be done well if you're consciously thinking about every stroke or are worried about the future consequences. There's simply not time for your brain to rationally process all the available information, and if you try it's likely that you'll suffer 'paralysis through analysis' when your muscles tighten up and you start to hesitate with your strokes.

That's why Decision Making is so important – because it ensures you think consciously about your performance in advance and then, through mental rehearsal, prime yourself to Execute automatically 'in the moment'. This requires that you can trust and let go when you Execute, because technical thoughts will just interfere with your performance. This doesn't mean that you stop thinking completely during a competition. In longer events like a marathon race you need to monitor what's going on around you and respond, and even in a short event like a slalom you will need to stay alert to changes and quickly seize an opportunity. The difference is that decisions made while you're in Execution should be tactical not technical. Tactical thinking is about *what* to do, like a choice to accelerate past a competitor who's stumbling on a portage, or to take a faster line into an upstream gate that appears when an eddy surges. Technical thinking is about *how* you do something, and if you start doing this during a performance the chances are you'll probably be less fluid in your actions. At worst, you'll lose your focus completely and make a serious mistake.[15]

**Real world example**

Jamie McEwan writes of his experience solo paddling the Chattooga River in 1971. It's a powerful and vivid description of Execution, being totally absorbed in the river's flow:

*"I looked up at the sky, around at the undramatic brown hills, and felt a crazy, disconnected freedom. I could scream, sing, shout, run naked... No one was there; no one would pass this way for months. How strange it seemed, that of all of the places on Earth, I was in this particular one. I looked back up the river. No trace remained of my passage. Yet here I was, somehow. Still shivering.*

*Looking back at the drop I saw, in one sweeping glance, the proper line. I imagined how it would feel, how the strokes would fall, how the waves would jostle me. Then, without ever having come to a conscious decision, I trotted back to my boat.*

*Swooping with the water as it curved, then smacking into the boiling pool below, seemed so natural, so inevitable, that it was almost dreamlike. The imagined run and the experience had blended. More rapids, more drops, more decisions. Rocks and water, hills and sky were my only audience. All the attention I would have given to companions fell only on these – and on myself."[16]*

# Attributes of great Execution

A paddler with well-developed Execution demonstrates these four attributes:

**In the moment attention**

Be here now. This sounds so simple, but most of the time our attention is not here and not now – either we're revisiting the past or worrying about the future. Paddlers who can be fully present, no matter what they're doing, can translate this into focused, in the moment attention during a competitive performance or on a crunch point on a river.

**Delivers under pressure**

The ability to execute under pressure is honed through many hours of deliberate, high quality practice. This means narrowing the gap between training and competition so that you've put yourself under the same pressure many, many times in training before you come to race. Of course not every training session can or should replicate a competition, but the more you practise executing your skills under the clock, or in head-to-head racing, the better prepared you will be to Execute on the big day.

*"I try to enjoy racing, to have fun, to do things I do every day in training and I don't try to do anything special. A couple of years ago I tried to do something special and be really good in races, but now I just do what I do every*

*day and what I do best and I think this makes it easier."*

**Corinna Kuhnle, 2010 and 2011 Women's K1 World Slalom Champion**[17]

*Sportscene / R van Bommel*

## Deals with distractions

Great performers have learned how to mentally switch on from the start of the competitive phase and maintain a high level of commitment throughout their event regardless of other competitors, external events or even mistakes that they have made. They can quickly re-focus when a distraction causes a loss of attention. Mastery Motivation has an important role to play here, because it provides the discipline and commitment to stick to your performance rather than give up.

## Adaptable to late changes

Although Execution relies on well-honed skills, this doesn't mean mindless robotic paddling. Great paddlers can respond creatively to opportunities as they emerge, whether that's a new piece of information delivered by your coach while you sit on the start-line, or the discovery that the line down a rapid that looked fine from 30 metres up the bank is blocked by a submerged tree. In either case successful Execution (and even survival) requires a paddler to quickly re-assess and respond.

# Warning signs

Here are some signs that suggest a paddler needs to work on their Execution.

**The paddler**

- Loses concentration in training or competition, especially following an error. A completely error-free performance is a worthy aspiration for anyone, but the reality is that there will always be moments where a race or line down a rapid doesn't quite go to plan. A paddler who responds badly to small mistakes can throw away a whole performance. Even worse is a loss of temper or abandoning a run completely;

- Suffers from 'paralysis through analysis' and tightens up physically. This happens when a paddler starts to think too much during, or just before, a run and stops trusting their skills and experience. It shows up as hesitant, jerky paddling and tight movements;

- Performs better in training than competition. This is also a sign that a paddler needs to improve Mastery Motivation, because thinking has moved to the future outcome rather than the immediate performance.

# Summary - Execution

Execution is your ability to focus intently and deliver your performance under pressure. At times it might lead to a state of peak experience known as flow, in which everything seems effortless. But regardless of how you feel, you need to be able to focus, commit to your plan and adapt as necessary. This is easier to do consistently when you have trained well and ask no more of yourself in competition than you have in practice.

**Your learning**

What helps you get into an Execution mindset?

How do you stay focused during training or competition?

---

13. Quoted to me by Australian junior slalom coach Peter Eckhardt

14. The term flow was coined by psychologist Mihály Csikszentmihalyi and has since been used by many performance psychologists and others

15. See Daniel Kahneman's book Thinking, Fast and Slow for more on how the brain works in two very different ways. His model of System 1 thinking is what you use during Execution, System 2 thinking in Decision Making

16. http://www.sitezed.com/jamie-mcewan-ii-years-later-i-added-the-frame-chattooga-river-1971/

17. http://www.sportscene.tv/whitewater/canoe-slalom/competitions/2011-icf-world-championships-canoe-slalom/articles/interview-with-corinna-kuhnle

# Chapter 4
## Teamwork

*"We worked very hard to realise that these guys (the silver medal winning C2 crew of Florence and Hounslow) were our greatest asset, because through their presence, their quality, they would force us, push us, make us learn to cope with a pressured environment every day. They would be there every day and we would be there every day, we saw they would give us what we lacked in the previous Olympic environment."*

**Etienne Stott, C2 Slalom Gold Medallist London 2012**[18]

Teamwork is your ability to build and maintain relationships, offer and receive support from teammates, and contribute to an effective team environment. It requires the skills to give and receive feedback and the ability to be honest with yourself and others.

You might be surprised that Teamwork is a fundamental requirement in paddle sports. After all, 'to paddle your own canoe' is a cliché for wanting to be independent and remain separate from a group. It's true that most paddlers value their autonomy and like to be in control of their own performance. Many paddlers were exposed to team sports at school, and it's typical that they either didn't enjoy relying on other people, or having other people rely on them. And most of the competitive paddle-sport disciplines emphasize individual rather than collective results apart from canoe polo, rafting, K2 and K4 crew boats and slalom and sprint C2. Yet most competitive paddlers train and compete within some form of team environment, even if it is a small, tight unit of a paddler and coach. In a well-funded Olympic discipline a paddler might well interact off the water with a technical coach, physiotherapist, performance analyst, strength and conditioning coach, psychologist, nutritionist and so on. I've seen examples in both slalom and sprint where the right team environment has helped individual paddlers push themselves and each other to greater heights, through highly competitive training and a challenging team culture. Many coaches believe that a centralised training system where you have plenty of group training is the best, quickest way to develop a lot of good athletes on a continuing basis – yet there are also plenty of examples of paddlers achieving success much more independently.

Out on a river or the sea there are those who prefer to paddle solo, but most of the time you paddle and travel in a group for reasons of safety and practicality. Being part of a strong, harmonious team is an important source of self-confidence, especially when conditions are tough. And sadly we can probably all think of times when tense interactions amongst a paddling group have been more difficult than dealing with a new stretch of whitewater!

From a psychological point of view, Teamwork requires you to access very different states of mind than Mastery Motivation, Execution and Decision Making. These Fundamentals all require you to be focused on yourself more than on others, and to strive for self-control and discipline. Teamwork requires you to change so that, at the right times, you focus more and on providing care and support to other people. This is why Teamwork can be challenging for some paddlers, because it takes them out of their natural comfort zone, and out of the state of mind that they need to thrive in the heat of training and competition. Some will choose to paddle and train alone, others will learn how to develop motivational flexibility – the ability to move between a focus on themselves and a concern for others. There are real advantages to learning how to work effectively with other people, both on the water and in your career and with your family.

### Real life example

I remember when I was in my early twenties and fully focused on pursuing my slalom career, my sister said to me, "You're not a very nice person anymore." I was momentarily shocked. In my mind, I was simply and clearly focused on doing all that I could to qualify for the Australian team and then successfully race overseas. To me this was self-evidently a good thing to do and I assumed that anyone who knew me would surely be entirely supportive, adaptable and tolerant of my actions. I had never really considered the impact my endeavours might have on anyone else. With all the arrogance of youth I quickly discounted her feedback and maintained my focus on canoeing.

It was only when I moved on to coach young athletes and learned a bit more about psychology that I fully realised what was going on. High level, sustained success in sport requires certain characteristics like intense focus, aggression, commitment, self-belief and even obsession. These attitudes are all to do with achieving *mastery* over oneself, the sport and one's competitors. Admirable as they may be in competitive sport, taken to an extreme in daily life they are more typical of a sociopath. These characteristics are the opposite of being caring, empathic, nurturing and kind – which psychologically are all to do with *sympathy*. Mastery and sympathy are two important motivations that we need to be able to access appropriately so that our state of mind, emotions and goals are aligned with the context. Racing in the sympathy state is a recipe for disaster, just as is trying to be a loving parent while in the mastery state. Effective Teamwork means being able to make these motivational changes between mastery and sympathy, self and others, at the right time.

# Attributes of great Teamwork

Paddlers with well-developed Teamwork demonstrate these three attributes:

**They support and encourage their teammates.**

Being in a positive, successful group can help each individual perform better than they would alone, and the simplest way to foster this is to encourage each other. Whether that's cheering on their teammates, or simply offering a quiet word of support, paddlers with well-developed Teamwork are confident enough to give a little to others.

**They appreciate their coaches and support staff.**

A simple 'thank you' is a small yet powerful gesture to the coach who arrived in the dark then stood in the freezing cold for an hour. A quiet word of thanks to the volunteer gate judge at the end of a local race goes a long way in sustaining their contribution. Even

*Sportscene / R van Bommel*

professional staff like acknowledgement from time to time. And remember that this is not all for their benefit – it will increase your success too. Professional support staff will never admit to it, but the reality is that people like helping likeable people.

**They put the team's needs above their own when necessary.**

This requires a careful balancing. In a competitive environment there are times when it's necessary to be single-minded and even stubborn. But there are also times when a small compromise can have a much bigger benefit for the group as a whole. Mature paddlers have learned how to give and take.

*"One of the most admirable characteristics of the kayaking community is this: when someone is in trouble, anyone present will step up and in an instant put his or her own life at risk to save a complete stranger. On a more pedestrian level, paddlers are almost always there for each other when it comes time to help someone who's swam or unpin a boat, even if it isn't a life threatening situation."*

**Louis Geltman, Oregon based whitewater kayaker writing on Site Zed[19]**

# Warning signs

There are a number of signs that suggest that paddlers need to develop better Teamwork.

**Paddlers**

- Behave selfishly and consistently put their needs above those of the team. Never willing to compromise, their rigidity soon builds resentment and people start to withdraw their good will;

- Create or fuel conflict in the team by complaining, whining or bitching about other people behind their backs. When challenged to express a concern openly, they will often claim they were simply misunderstood and back down rather than face conflict openly;

- React defensively and are not open to feedback. This makes it difficult to talk in an open and constructive way about behaviour;

- Are dismissive or disrespectful towards coaches or support staff. Always ready to complain about someone else's weakness, they are slow to praise and rarely say 'thanks'.

# Summary - Teamwork

Teamwork is based on your ability to get on well with other people. It's critical in sport and in any walk of life. Some psychologists like Daniel Goleman[20] even argue that your level of emotional intelligence is the most important factor in life success. Canoe sport is a great vehicle for developing this life skill, because it relies on your ability to perform as an individual AND within a team.

**Your learning**

Think about the people who help you: coaches, parents, training partners, and sponsors... When was the last time you said 'thank you' to appreciate their efforts? When did you last ask how you could help them to help you?

**We've now introduced and defined the four Fundamentals that, together, create self-confidence. You've probably recognised that you already demonstrate them a lot naturally. In the next chapter, I describe some practical things you can do to develop your self-confidence and the Fundamentals even further.**

*AEphotos.co.uk / A Edmonds*

---

18.  http://www.youtube.com/watch?v=ok5GQ5hbV94

19.  http://www.sitezed.com/pushing-it/

20.  http://www.danielgoleman.info

# Chapter 5
## Developing the Fundamentals

*Carolyn Cooper*

## What you can do yourself

All paddlers possess the Fundamentals to some extent, so the first step is to recognise the skills you already use. Simply understanding the Fundamentals will help you develop them naturally alongside your physical and technical training. However, just as a naturally strong athlete will still benefit by lifting weights in the gym, so too can you enhance your psychological strengths by learning to adapt to the right performance demands in your training environment. This means deliberately building in opportunities that will test your ability to make decisions, to execute under pressure, to work with other people and to maintain your motivation. There's a beautiful example of this in Scott Shipley's book 'Every Crushing Stroke' in which he describes shovelling snow in bare feet at the end of a winter slalom training session – talk about building tough Mastery Motivation!

*Our toughness had a profound effect on our training. Despite the harsh Canadian winters our training totals were completely unaffected by the weather. If our training schedule said train, we trained; the weather had nothing to do with it. Our mindset became one of our biggest strengths. No amount of effort was too much to ask if it might pry precious milliseconds off our times. We were of singular mind and indefatigable in our efforts – we had become the purest form of fanatics.*

**Scott Shipley, Every Crushing Stroke**[21]

There are also many techniques and skills that you can use to develop and strengthen the Fundamentals. I will describe some of them in this chapter, but this isn't a comprehensive list. I've chosen the skills that I have learned are the most effective and should form the core of your mental skills 'toolkit' that you can use throughout your career.

# The coach's role

A coach has an important role to play to maintain the necessary focus on the psychological Fundamentals as well as on race tactics, physical conditioning and technique. It's worth noting that the coaching philosophy I'm advocating is based on my personal values of wanting to develop athletes' autonomy so they learn to take responsibility for their own development, and on my experience working primarily with paddlers from western cultures (Britain, Australia, New Zealand, Canada). Not all coaches work from the same values, and there are very different approaches in different sports and across different cultures. Some coaches will take a much more authoritarian approach in which they dictate what the athlete should do, and the athlete's job is simply to comply and deliver results. My personal view is that an authoritarian coaching approach works best in those sports, or paddle-sport disciplines, that require a highly predictable performance in a stable environment, like swimming, rowing or sprint kayaking. I'm not convinced that an authoritarian coaching style prepares paddlers to perform in a more complex competitive environment where more independent thinking is required, such as slalom or freestyle.

*Sportscene / R van Bommel*

# Working with a sport psychologist

I know that some paddlers are sceptical of working with a psychologist, believing that seeing a 'shrink' is a sign of weakness. Some have had bad experiences with poorly trained or unethical practitioners, so I can appreciate a sense of caution. I also know that sport psychologists have helped successful, medal-winning athletes in pretty much every sport all across the world. So what should you look for in an effective sport psychologist to make sure you benefit?

*Here are four things you should consider:*

## 1. Training and accreditation

Many countries now require that sport psychologists fulfil both academic and professional training and maintain formal accreditation. This means that a sport psychologist will have studied to post-graduate level, have developed skills under the guidance of a more experienced practitioner, and maintain ongoing professional learning. This gives you some assurance that a person is competent, but it's still important to ask about the psychologist's training and find out how relevant it is for your needs. A solid grounding in psychology, sport science and counselling is an ideal mix.

## 2. Empathy and trustworthiness

You need to be able to build a trusting relationship with your sport psychologist. So it's important that he or she can listen well and show that they understand you. Pay attention to their personal qualities, how they speak and listen to others, how they handle themselves under pressure, and how they talk about their other clients. Ethical sport psychologists will maintain professional boundaries, which means that they won't gossip about clients or reveal things that were said in confidence.

## 3. Experience of your sport

It's not essential that a sport psychologist has been, or is currently, a paddler to work effectively with paddlers. While it can help to have a close appreciation of your discipline from the start, good sport psychologists are fast learners and will often add value by asking 'naïve' questions that can helpfully challenge your assumptions. What is essential is that they understand high performance sport and ideally have their own direct experience of being a competitor or coach. It doesn't matter what their sport is, and cross-fertilization from different sports or paddle sport disciplines can be really helpful.

## 4. Working style

There are three main working approaches that sport psychologists will use, often in combination. Each has its place and there are advantages and disadvantages to each. Understanding these options will make it easier to agree the best way of working with a sport psychologist in your situation.

*Here are the three most common methods:*

a)  Work directly with the paddler
b)  Work with the paddler and coach together
c)  Work with a whole squad or team

Working directly with a paddler is the simplest approach. The psychologist can focus on understanding the paddler's individual needs and then help them to develop and apply specific skills. This works fine if the paddler isn't part of a squad or doesn't have a coach to help them with other aspects of their training. There can be problems, however, if there isn't close alignment between the coach and the sport psychologist. This can lead to the paddler getting contradictory messages from the coach and psychologist. Some coaches can even feel threatened by a paddler forming a close relationship with someone other than them.

To overcome this, psychologists can choose to work with the paddler and coach together. This makes it easier to get alignment and can serve to strengthen the relationship between paddler and coach. Given that most paddlers spend more time with their coach than a psychologist, the coach can also reinforce key messages and behaviours in daily training sessions. It's a little more complicated to work with two people together so it's more demanding on the psychologist, and there are times when a paddler may appreciate being able to speak in confidence to someone who is NOT their coach.

Increasingly, sport psychologists will work at a systemic level with a whole team or programme. In this role they will help coaches, support staff and managers to work together effectively, paying attention to the team culture, leadership and communication. This is potentially a very powerful role to play, as it can have a major impact on a whole team. It does require specific consulting skills that are not often taught in conventional sport psychology training, as well as the maturity and credibility to positively influence a wide range of people.

# Developing Mastery Motivation

To develop Mastery Motivation, a **coach** can

- Reward and reinforce the right attitude and effort as well as the outcomes that a paddler achieves;

- Talk with the paddler to help them develop a healthy attitude to competition; teach paddlers to value mastery over the skills of their discipline rather than just race results or beating opponents;

- Set and maintain a high standard of professionalism, eg being on time, being well prepared, reviewing thoroughly and prioritising training;

- Design training sessions that are particularly difficult and physically challenging, and be explicit that they are designed to develop Mastery Motivation as well as strength and fitness;

- Collate a video of a paddler's highlights and best performances, and then have them watch it before a major competition;

- Encourage paddlers to take responsibility for their lifestyle, physical recovery and diet.

## Goal Setting

*Ah, but a man's reach should exceed his grasp,*
*Or what's a heaven for?*

**Andrea del Sarto, by  Robert Browning**

As a paddler, one of the most important things you can do to develop your Mastery Motivation is to challenge yourself to set higher standards by using a range of goals. Goals need to be stretching enough to challenge you, but close enough so that you believe you can achieve them. It takes time to learn how to get the right level of stretch and it's a highly individual process. For a young paddler, it's often better to take a series of small, more easily achievable steps to build momentum and confidence. Other paddlers, typically those who are more experienced and confident, will only be satisfied when they are pursuing big, audacious goals. A coach can help you to look objectively at your past and current performances, talk through the options, and get a realistic sense of how long it takes to develop in your discipline. Remember though that goals are more powerful, compelling and effective when you choose and commit to them yourself – rather than trying to meet other people's expectations. So if you are working with a coach, make sure the goals are yours and not your coach's!

There are three different types of goals and great performers use all of them in combination, because they tap into different sources of motivation. They are Outcome, Performance and Process goals:

## Outcome Goals

*Such as:*

- Winning a medal
- Achieving a top ten season's ranking
- Making the final of a big race
- Paddling a particular river or sea crossing

Outcome goals are usually visible and involve comparison with other competitors. Because they are public, they can be a source of pressure if a paddler gets too focused on the implications of failure or the fruits of success. They are also hard to control because achieving them is influenced by other competitors' performances. They can be highly motivational because they are tangible and easily understood by people outside the sport. An effective outcome goal will be a long-term source of motivation that gets you out of bed on a cold winter morning to go training.

## Performance Goals

*Such as:*

- Scoring a certain number of points on a freestyle ride
- Beating your Personal Best time for the 1000 metres
- Getting within a nominated percentage of the fastest boat in a slalom race

Performance goals are measurable and objective, and are often determined by the stopwatch. They can help you assess your progress towards your outcome goals and, ideally, are totally within your control and not based only on comparison with other paddlers.

## Process Goals

*Such as:*

- Maintaining your desired paddling cadence through the phases of a 1000-metre sprint race
- Keeping your boat flat on the entry to every upstream gate
- Nailing your line and keeping your deck dry through each major rapid in an extreme race
- Getting good rotation and leading with your head in a freestyle ride
- Maintaining the run of your ski during the down-wind leg of an ocean race

Process goals keep you focused on important elements of your technique or race plan. You will often focus on them extensively in training. When executed well, process goals will help you achieve your performance and outcome goals. They may rely more on feel and be harder to measure than performance or outcome goals, so you may need to rely on feedback from your coach or video.

Ideally you will see a clear flow between your outcome goals (what you want to achieve) with your performance goals (the evidence that you are on track) and your process goals (the actual behaviours and technique that you are refining in your training). Different goals become important at different stages of the season – generally the closer you are to competing, the more important it is to focus on your process goals rather than the outcome. Many people find it distracting to be thinking about the outcome when they're sitting on the start-line, and prefer to be more focused on their first couple of strokes.

### Which goals are most important – the outcome or the process?

Would you rather win a race with a poor performance, or execute your race perfectly and finish fourth? This is a question that often leaves paddlers feeling confused about what goals to pursue, and it points to some important aspects of your motivation.

*There's an old story of a Japanese Samurai warrior who was sent out by his master to capture and execute a dangerous thief. The warrior tracked the thief with great difficulty for several days over remote country and eventually cornered him. As the warrior raised his sword, the brigand insultingly spat in his face. The warrior felt a flash of anger and paused. He then lowered his sword and walked away. He chose not to kill the thief at that moment, because feeling angry was the wrong motivation for a Samurai warrior to take a life. Once composed, he later caught the thief and completed his task.*

At its most ideal, Mastery Motivation is a desire to compete with a pure heart, focused only on executing your own performance with skill, strength and courage so you paddle to the very best of your own ability. Any deviation from this intent is likely to weaken your capacity to be fully focused. However, the reality is that most of us will struggle to achieve and maintain this level of motivational clarity. So it's helpful to realise that, for most of us, it takes time to develop Mastery Motivation. There are three common beliefs that stand in the way:

1. We believe that the outcome is more important than the quality of the performance
2. We believe that beating our opponents will make us a better person
3. We believe that achieving competitive success will make other people like us more.

The first belief is understandable because results count, and in competitive sport (unlike the life of a Samurai warrior) there are many times when it's better to 'win ugly' than 'lose pretty'. While there's no denying that results are important, the trick is to keep them in perspective and think about your outcome goals in the right way, and at the right time. Dreaming of winning a gold medal can be a powerful motivation and inspire the hard work necessary to make it real. But the closer the actual competition comes, the more important it is to channel your motivation and focus on the task at hand, not the future outcome.

Notice how champion slalom paddler Daniele Molmenti describes his experience when he thought about the consequences of a big race on the start-line:

*I was very nervous before (the start of the 2011 world championships). During the warm-up I thought that it was the only chance for Italy to get an Olympic quota, so I wanted to do it. I didn't take any risk to be sure to finish in the first fifteen. In the end I did a good time, but I didn't feel really good this morning to be honest. The goal of the day is reached, the goal for the nation. Now I have my personal goal, it's to beat my opponents and get a new world medal. It will be hard to get the gold again, because they are really good. I didn't do a really good jump. If I do, I can finish first, of course."*

**Daniele Molmenti, twice K1 slalom World Champion and Olympic Gold Medallist**[22]

The weight of having to achieve an Olympic qualifying place led to Daniele feeling very nervous, not feeling good and not taking risks. It was an external goal, one he carried on behalf of his country, which contrasted with his personal goal of winning a medal. It's long been known that being too focused on the consequences of the outcome impairs performance. Here's some advice from a Chinese philosopher writing more than 2000 years ago:

*When an archer is shooting for nothing he has all his skill.
If he shoots for a brass buckle he is already nervous. If he
shoots for a prize of gold he goes blind or sees two targets
– he is out of his mind! His skill has not changed. But the
prize divides him. He cares. He thinks more of winning
than of shooting and the need to win drains him of power.*

**Chuang Tzu (300 BC), 29,4**

The other common attitudes – believing that beating your
opponents will make you a better person and believing that
achieving success will make other people like you more – can be
harder to recognise and even tougher to admit. It's easy to rely on
sporting success to boost self-esteem, because success can lead to
praise, affirmation and confidence that might be lacking elsewhere
in your life. Feeling unloved or unworthy can create a powerfully
obsessive drive to excel at sport but is also a fragile source of
confidence. When your results slip or you have a bad race, your
self-confidence can come crashing down too. Low self-confidence
then makes it harder to compete well at your next race, so there's a
risk of getting into a downward spiral. So the most robust source of

self-confidence and satisfaction comes from within, not just from achieving results. Psychologists call this intrinsic motivation, and it's an important component of Mastery Motivation.

It can be a life's work to really learn how to compete with the Samurai warrior's emotional clarity and be content with seeking your ultimate run, not just chasing results or trying to meet other people's expectations. This is why it's important to have a good working relationship with a coach or sport psychologist who can help you to develop intrinsic Mastery Motivation over time. Doing so will pay big benefits in your whole life, not just on the water because you are more likely to seek and find a meaningful career and maintain healthy relationships when you are 'comfortable in your own skin'.

Consider these words from Dave Florence on winning Gold in C1 and C2 at the 2013 World Slalom Championships:

*"This weekend the results came about not from me chasing a result or trying to win the double. It was trying to put in the best runs I could on the days. I focused on that and it's gone well for me and that's what I'll continue to do."*[23]

## Goal-setting questions

What are the most important outcomes you'd like to achieve in your paddling career?

What are your Performance Goals, the stepping-stones that will show you are making progress towards your Outcome goals?

What's a realistic, but challenging timescale to achieve these performances and outcomes?

In order to achieve these Performances, what skills must you master? (Think about the technical, physical, mental and environmental demands of your event.)

*Sportscene / R van Bommel*

# Developing Decision Making

If you're a **coach,** here's what you can do to help your paddlers develop Decision Making:

- Ensure that your paddlers practise different techniques and tactics in training sessions. Don't get stuck in a rut!

- Teach your paddlers to systematically evaluate different options and educate them so they can make good choices on their own;

- Provide paddlers with objective feedback (especially video) after training or competition to help them to evaluate their own performance;

- Create training scenarios where paddlers must make fast

choices or respond to unexpected changes – then review the effectiveness of their decisions;

- Ensure that paddlers develop, apply and review a competition plan;

- Help them to take responsibility for their long-term training and development; educate them about periodization, nutrition and the importance of sleep so they can make informed choices.

As a paddler there are two specific things you can do to develop your Decision Making – use a *training journal* and refine your *mental rehearsal skills*.

## 1. Record your plan and then monitor your progress in a training journal.

This sounds so simple yet I'm amazed at the number of paddlers who don't maintain a simple training journal. It seems that as paddlers get older they come to rely more on their experience and less on a formal plan. Although I can understand this sentiment, there's a risk that your training will be compromised because you won't have the data to back up your intuition. Of course many coaches will keep detailed training records and make them available to their paddlers – this achieves the same outcome of enabling their paddlers to think objectively about what they are doing.

Here are some of the ways you can use a training journal:

- Write down your goals for your career and for the season ahead. Use your journal to keep them visible to you, and add some pictures. Experiment with your computer screen saver, or at least a photo that stays on your screensaver or mobile phone, to provide a visual reminder of your goals.

- Write down your annual, monthly and weekly training plan. If a coach provides your training plan, ask him or her to explain why you're training the way you are. Take responsibility and get curious about what you're doing – don't just passively receive a training plan.

- Record what training you actually do. Where it's different from your plan, make a note of why this happened. Were you more tired than you expected? Or did you have more energy? Was it because of someone else's actions? This will help you refine your own self-awareness and judgment.

- Keep track of your body weight, hours of sleep and resting pulse rate. Make a note of when you get ill or catch a cold. Often an illness is preceded by an increase in resting heart rate or less sleep, and if this is true for you spotting the warning signs can help you rest up earlier.

- Write a review of each competition to assess how well your race plan is working, and then use this to inform your subsequent training. It's also very useful to track your competitive progress over the year against your performance and outcome goals.

And if you're not into competition, it's just as useful to keep notes or a blog about your river or sea kayaking trips. Make a note of the river level, tidal conditions, time taken, who was on the trip and any notable features. You'll be surprised by how valuable it is to look back on your notes when it comes to planning your next trip to the same location.

## 2. Develop confidence in mental rehearsal

*"What the mind conceives the body achieves"*

Mental rehearsal is based on the premise that an imagined experience generates many of the same neurological and muscular pathways as the real experience. This means that an athlete who imagines taking a paddle stroke shows the same brain and muscle responses as one who actually does it. Athletes in all sports regularly use mental rehearsal in a wide range of situations:

- To improve self-confidence
- To prepare for a specific opponent or competition
- To increase concentration
- To practise dealing with difficulties within an event
- To speed up skill acquisition
- To aid recovery from injury

**Top Tips for Effective Mental Rehearsal**

There are two key ways to use mental rehearsal. You can find a quiet, non-distracting environment, assume a comfortable position and relax with simple breathing exercises before using your imagination. Or you can practise it dynamically, moving your body as if you were really paddling. There's some evidence that dynamic practice is more effective, but whichever method you prefer make sure you make the rehearsal as vivid as possible.[24]

- Identify which of the senses (sight, sound or feel) work best for you – we have different preferences – and try to include as many as possible. The more vivid your experience is, the better, and it seems that the most important aspect is the feel of the movement.

- Try varying the visual perspective: use an internal perspective where you are 'in' the scene looking out, as well as being a 'third person' observer.

- Pay attention to felt sense, to capture both how your body feels, as well how you want to feel emotionally.

- Do the rehearsal in real time. This can help prevent daydreaming and getting caught in an imagery loop where you repeat over and over again. If you're rehearsing a very specific move, use a stopwatch and compare your rehearsed time with the real thing.

- Be as specific as possible and have very precise objectives. This is especially important in an event like slalom, where the paddler must place the boat in exactly the right place and at the right speed at key places on the course.

- Focus on the positive – experience yourself being successful rather than failing!

- Short regular practice sessions (five to ten minutes) are generally more effective than longer, less focused attempts. Like anything, you get better at it with practice; so don't give up after a few failed attempts.

**Frequently Asked Questions**

*What's the difference between Imagery and Mental Rehearsal?*

Both rely on using your imagination to improve performance. Mental rehearsal is often used to practise a specific skill in a highly realistic way or to test out different options. Imagery is more imaginative, and taps into your brain's creative hemisphere. For example, I once helped an athlete develop his Mastery Motivation. I asked him to describe what it felt like when he was really confident and in top form, then to find an image that represented this. Sitting quietly, in a relaxed state, he came up with the image of a medieval knight in armour ready for battle. So we used this image to help him tap into his Mastery Motivation before an event. As well as mentally rehearsing key aspects of his performance, he'd also imagine himself wearing a suit of armour, feeling strong and ready for a fight.

*I close my eyes but can't see anything – it's all a blank.*

People vary in their ability to create mental images, but it's a skill that improves with practice. Start with some simple drills before moving onto more complex rehearsals. For example, sit quietly and look at an everyday item – like a coffee cup. Close your eyes and visualise the image, then open your eyes to look at it again. Keep repeating till you can hold the image in your mind.

*I start off well, but my performance goes terribly wrong and I can't seem to create a positive image.*

Let the negative image run, but change it from colour to black and white, then see if you can shrink it down in your imagination so that it disappears completely. Are you attempting a performance too far beyond your ability? Try the imagery again with a less ambitious outcome and build from there.

*I lose focus and start daydreaming, or drift off to sleep.*

Are you sitting or lying down when you rehearse? Try sitting upright on a straight-backed chair. Keep your practice sessions short – a couple of minutes can be plenty if you're picking out the key aspects of your performance. If you are mentally rehearsing your performance, try 'dynamic rehearsal', when you're sitting in your boat or on dry land, holding your paddle and doing the strokes as you imagine them.

*I rehearsed the situation fine, but when I got to it in real life it was completely different. I tried to make my responses fit with my mental rehearsal, but it turned out badly.*

In a contest between your expectations and reality, reality always wins. Never let your expectations or emotions get in the way of dealing with what is actually going on. Remember that Execution is about being in the present moment – not the images created in your mind. Make sure that next time you imagine yourself dealing with a range of situations, not just your preferred outcome. That way you can be more responsive and adapt to the real demands more quickly.

# Developing Execution

To develop Execution, a **coach** can

- Make sure that your paddlers physically AND mentally warm up – don't begin training until they are focused and ready to deliver;

- Keep the quality of training high, and don't allow paddlers to abandon runs even if they make a mistake;

- Design training sessions that replicate competition. In slalom this means timed and scored runs, and sessions in which the paddler does a single full-length run with bankside preparation. Freestyle paddlers can do 45 second timed and scored rides, with a ten to fifteen minute break between each one. Sprint paddlers can do sessions that replicate warming up then a single effort over the relevant distance;

- Design training sessions that replicate performance under pressure or in the face of distractions. In slalom, aim for clean sessions (ie ones with no gate touches for the entire session). Set up speakers playing loud music during a freestyle or sprint session and have someone do a live and distracting commentary.

## Mindfulness

The main challenge to good Execution comes from distractions that pop up as random thoughts or occur in response to an error. These thoughts will often take your attention into the future – "I'll never win now" – or into the past – "If only I hadn't made that mistake" – and away from the 'here and now' of the immediate moment. Preventing distractions from occurring is pretty difficult, if not impossible. *Mindfulness* practice is a really effective way of getting better at improving your concentration and quickly re-focusing when distractions occur.[25] I recommend Mindfulness to all my corporate and sports clients as the most effective way of learning to be 'in the moment' and fully present.

Sportscene / R van Bommel

Mindfulness is the skill of maintaining your focus on the task at hand. It is simple but not easy. Simple, because to practise requires no more than to sit quietly, close your eyes and bring your attention to your breathing. Not easy, because you will quickly realise that your mind is full of thoughts, both pleasant daydreams and worries, that will take your attention away before you know it. The act of mindfulness isn't reaching a blissful, spaced out state of mind – it's the discipline of *noticing* a thought or feeling, without getting carried away by it, and gently and persistently *bringing your attention back* to your breathing. Some people prefer to focus on repeating a short word or phrase (known as a mantra) instead of their breathing. Either approach can work fine and is a matter of personal preference.

It is possible to be present and mindful at any time, doing any activity. Don't confuse mindfulness with being passive and low energy. When you sit quietly and pay attention to your breathing, a natural side effect is to feel calm and relaxed. But the important thing that you are doing in this exercise is to train your attention, not just to chill out. Think of sessions like this as the equivalent of a gym session for your mental concentration and ability to Execute well. Whatever thought or feeling arises, you just notice it and come back to your breathing. In more active settings it's just the same, except that instead of returning attention to your breath you return it to the task at hand – so if you're paddling this might be the line for the next gate, a key stroke over a wave or focusing on your torso rotation and reach.

**Mindfulness Practice off the water**

This simple exercise will help develop the skill of mindful attention. Start by practising for five minutes a day and then extend to fifteen to twenty minutes per day. It's best to set a timer so you don't have to open your eyes to check the time. There are several neat smartphone Apps that do this well; I use one called Equanimity. As you practise you'll find that it gets easier to focus on your breathing for longer before thoughts come up, but this will probably vary from day to day. The key is to stick with it, be patient with yourself, and accept that you won't 'get it right'. Accept that you will have distracting thoughts, and remember that you are developing the skill to quickly notice a distracting thought and bring your attention back to your breathing.

*Find a quiet, comfortable sitting position. Notice the position of your feet, arms, and hands. Allow your eyes to close gently. Begin by noticing what you can hear around you, the temperature of the room, the sensations in your body. Gently bring your attention inwards to your breathing. Don't try to change your breathing or deliberately slow it down, just notice the air moving in and out of your lungs all by itself. As you sit quietly like this, you'll soon notice that thoughts and feelings will come up – perhaps you'll start thinking about your next training session or what you'll eat for lunch. Perhaps you'll be asking yourself how long you have to keep doing this for. Perhaps you'll find yourself wandering off on a pleasant daydream. This is normal. Don't get upset at yourself for losing concentration. Just patiently name the thought and gently bring your attention back to your breathing. Follow your breath, in and out. Just notice a distraction when it arises and bring your attention back to your breath.*

## Mindfulness Practice while Paddling

You can also develop mindfulness while you're paddling. Start when you're doing a simple flat-water session so you don't have too much going on with slalom gates or moving water. The aim of the practice is to bring your attention to what you are experiencing 'in the moment'.

*As you paddle, gently bring your attention to your body; notice how you are moving. Feel yourself breathing naturally. Feel your blade grip the water; notice how you twist and pull. Look at the bow of your boat and notice its movement. Become aware of the sounds you can hear; listen to your paddle and boat slicing through the water, or any other sounds in your environment. Feel the breeze or the sun on your body. Notice when your mind starts to wander. You may find yourself thinking about something that is not happening right now – either you are thinking back into the past about something that's already happened, or into the future about something yet to occur. Don't be critical of yourself or your mind when it wanders. When this happens, simply catch the thought, name it and let it go, and bring your attention back to your immediate, here and now experience. Continue to paddle and just accept thoughts or worries as they arise, notice them, let them go, and bring your attention back to now.*

Set a timer on your watch so you do this for (say) five minutes, then paddle normally for a while before repeating a five-minute spell. Think of it as interval training for your mind.

# Developing Teamwork

Sportscene / R van Bommel

Here are some things that a **coach** can do to develop Teamwork:

- Explain what teamwork means in your discipline and how a healthy team environment can benefit everyone's performance;

- Set clear expectations about team behaviour on and off the water. Work with your paddlers to develop a simple set of agreements about how you will work together. This is called a Team Charter;

- Reward and reinforce positive examples of teamwork – and

act swiftly when anyone behaves in a way that contravenes
your agreements;

- Constructively challenge paddlers who don't demonstrate
  the right behaviours. Help them to understand the impact of
  their behaviour and learn how to respond differently;

- Be a good role model in the way you communicate, listen
  and give feedback. Try to be open and non-defensive and
  show that you listen to, and appreciate different points of
  view;

- Create appropriate opportunities for paddlers to socialise
  and get to know each other off the water. This is especially
  important if they will be travelling or living together.

## Clean language

Language shapes how we think and behave – so changing how you
speak is one of the most powerful ways to improve teamwork. Here
are four simple guidelines that will make a real difference to the
quality of your relationships and your ability to balance your own
needs and the needs of the team.

### 1. Take responsibility for what you need and how you feel, rather than blaming someone else.

This means starting a sentence with 'I' rather than 'you' or 'we'. Be
clear about what you need in a situation and be prepared to state
that clearly, accepting that this may be different from what other
people need, and that you may need to negotiate. Speaking as 'I'
also helps you to accept that your emotions are YOUR response to
something that's happened. All too often people forget this and
blame, criticize or attack others when they're upset or stressed. This

just fuels conflict and makes it harder to reach an objective and fair conclusion.

*Unhelpful*

"You were wrong to use my paddling gear without asking me."

*Helpful*

"I was really angry when you took my paddling gear without asking."

*Unhelpful*

"This is a rubbish training session and we're wasting time sitting around talking too much.

*Helpful*

"I want to put in a solid session today, and I'm frustrated that I'm not getting enough time on the water."

**2. Show you've listened.**

Communication isn't the message that you broadcast; it's the message that the other person receives. So show that you've listened and understood what the other person has said, particularly under stress or when the emotional temperature is rising. The simplest way is to re-state what you've heard them say – this doesn't mean you have to agree with them, but it will help you stay on the same page.

*Unhelpful*

*Sue:* "I'm not really enjoying this trip, and I don't really want to stay on the river any longer."

*Bill:* "That's crazy, we can't walk out here, the gorge is way too steep."

*Sue:* "Don't call me crazy, it was your stupid idea to do this section of the river."

*Bill:* "You were happy enough at the start of the trip..."

*Helpful*

Sue: "I'm not really enjoying this trip, and I don't really want to stay on the river any longer."

*Bill:* "So you're not feeling it today – are you saying we should walk out now?"

*Sue:* "No, not walk out. But maybe we can just slow the pace a little and check out the lines a bit more. I'm out of my comfort zone and need more time to see the lines."

*Bill:* "Sure, we can slow down. We're more than half way now and we've got plenty of daylight left..."

## 3. Be specific.

If you're giving feedback or raising a concern, be as specific as you can and give a clear, recent example. Don't make generalised complaints because the other person will quite rightly point to the exceptions.

*Unhelpful*

*Coach:* "You're never on time for training and we're always wasting time waiting for you."

*Paddler:* "But the traffic was bad today, and anyway I'm usually on time."

*Helpful*

*Coach:* "We agreed to be on the water at 8.30 am, and you arrived today at 9.00 am. That's the third time you've been late this week."

*Paddler:* "Ok, sorry about that. You're right, it's been a bad week for me for getting here on time."

**4. Make requests, not criticisms.**

Telling someone what they should or shouldn't do implies you're 'finger pointing' and blaming them. The response will either be an argument or sullen compliance. A more adult way of communicating is to make a request that clearly expresses what you need or want. Of course the other person may want to negotiate with you about this – making a request doesn't automatically mean the other person will, or should, comply. But you will have a more sensible conversation this way.

*Unhelpful*

*Coach:* "You're clearly not committed enough; you should turn up on time."

*Paddler:* "What do you mean I'm not committed? Of course I'm committed!" OR saying "Sorry" but on the inside silently saying, "what does he know, of course I'm committed, he doesn't appreciate what else I have to do in the mornings."

*Helpful*

*Coach:* "If you want to remain part of this training squad, I would like you to get here on time."

*Athlete:* "Ok, that's clear to me. Would it be possible to talk about starting the sessions a little later? Because I need to drop my brother off at college on the way here."

21. http://www.sportscene.tv/whitewater/canoe-slalom/news/every-crushing-stroke-the-olympic-revolution-part-x

22. *http://www.sportscene.tv/whitewater/canoe-slalom/competitions/2011-icf-world-championships-canoe-slalom/articles/athlete-quotes-from-todays-races*

23. *http://www.bbc.co.uk/sport/0/canoeing/24110031*

24. This is an excellent and up-to-date guide to the research evidence and best practice use of mental imagery: *http://www.bases.org.uk/Use-of-Mental-Imagery-in-Sport-Exercise-and-Rehabilitation-Contexts*

25. There are lots of resources available that explain the benefits of Mindfulness. Two of the best books are John Kabbat-Zinn, Wherever you go, there you are: Mindfulness meditation for everyday life. London, Piatkus, 2004 and Mindfulness: A practical guide to finding peace in a frantic world. By Williams & Penman, London, Piatkus, 2011.

# Section I Review

So we've now introduced the four Fundamentals – Mastery
Motivation, Execution, Decision Making and Teamwork. If you've
read this far, you should have a pretty clear idea of what each
Fundamental is, and what a coach or paddler can do to develop
each one. Whatever aspect of the sport you enjoy, the Fundamentals
work together to give you the mental skills to feel self-confident and
perform at your best.

**The Fundamentals – Putting it all together**

1.  Reflect on your best ever performance in a competition, or
    on a great experience on a river or the sea. How did the four
    Fundamentals contribute to your self-confidence?

2.  After a training session or a recreational trip, give yourself
    a score out of 10 for each of the Fundamentals. Identify
    one thing you can do differently next time you paddle to
    improve your mental skills.

3.  Think of a way to strengthen your weakest fundamental,
    either when you're training or off the water. For example,
    learning to juggle is a great way of developing Execution.
    Doing really tough gym sessions can strengthen Mastery
    Motivation. Giving positive feedback to another paddler
    strengthens Teamwork.

# SECTION 2
# Chapter 6
## Competition

Race day is like travelling on a journey during which you will pass through several stages. Depending on the format of the event and the number of disciplines you are paddling, you will go through several cycles of:

- Pre-Race: when you are preparing and warming up
- Competition: the time on the water from the start-line to the finish line
- After-race: cooling down, reviewing and recovering

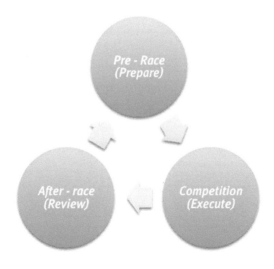

At each stage there are different challenges to meet. The most successful competitors are the ones who are best prepared to meet these demands – whether they come from your competitors, the scale of the event or the river itself. Your task is to be very clear about what the challenges are in your event and how you are going to meet them. Different people will have their own approaches to racing and choose to meet their challenges in their own way, so not everyone has to do the same thing or follow the same rigid plan. In fact it's really important to be creative and adaptable because the world rarely goes according to plan!

Some of the challenges you face in competition will be physical, like the ability to accelerate your sprint kayak to its optimal speed and sustain this for the duration of your race. Your training in the gym and the hours of hard work on the water are designed to prepare your body for this demand.

Some are technical challenges, like getting off to a fast start in a sprint race, being able to nail an upstream gate and be heading downstream in less than two seconds, or being able to put together a series of compound moves in a freestyle event. Good coaching, video analysis and smart training will help you refine your skills to meet such technical demands.

And some of the demands are psychological, and these are the ones we will focus on here. Like being able to remain focused and calm on the start line, or making the right race plan and sticking to it under pressure, or dealing with the knowledge that 15 million people are watching you on TV as you compete in an Olympic final.

I believe that we all have a natural ability to adapt to challenges – that's what training is all about and it's also how the human race has evolved and learned to survive. You can accelerate this natural process by being really clear about the demands you will face on race day, and being equally clear about how the psychological

Fundamentals will help you to do so.

I've developed a way to describe your event's specific challenges in each of the Pre-Event, Competition and After-Race stages because it's not enough simply to have a capability – you must also be able to draw upon it at a particular *time*. I call this a Performance Demand Model (PDM) and it will help you learn how to manage yourself through the race day environment. You will use the four Fundamentals of Mastery Motivation, Decision Making, Execution and Teamwork to meet the psychological demands of your event.

*Sportscene / R van Bommel*

# The Performance Demand Model (PDM)

It's important to develop your own PDM, ideally working with your coach or team-mates. The first step is to agree how you will define your Pre-Race, Competition and Post Race stages, recognizing that you will rarely go through a single performance cycle in a competition. Moving through a sprint regatta, freestyle competition or a major slalom, each heat, semi final and final represents its own performance cycle. So you need to think about your event as a whole, as well as about each individual performance through heats, semi-finals and finals.

Use a big piece of paper or a flip chart and write up three headings: Pre-Race, Competition and Post-Race. Then for each stage, ask yourself: "What do I need to thinking about?" "How do I want to be feeling?" "Who do I need to be communicating with?" "What do I need to do?"

Remember that there may be times when you have to accept that you won't be feeling great before a race. Here's how European Slalom Champion Fiona Pennie described the night before her victory:

*"I had a terrible night's sleep last night...but that never seems to be an issue so I wasn't perturbed by that."*[26]

You can also think about potential problems or unexpected events. For example, 'what if the race start is delayed?' 'What if I break my paddle on my practice run?' 'What if I have an absolutely brilliant first run?' The idea isn't just to come up with all sorts of problems, but to be prepared for anything and to feel confident and focused on race day. When you've identified a problem, see if you can re-frame it so that it becomes a positive application. For example, you might start with 'Don't get distracted by crowds'. This would be re-framed as 'Keep focused on my own performance'. 'Don't get too nervous before warm up' would be reframed as 'stay calm and positive before warm up'.

Write your answers down on sticky notes and place them on your chart. When you've got them all written down, experiment with clustering the sticky notes into the four Fundamentals.

Here's an example PDM that shows how a slalom paddler will draw on the Fundamentals at different stages of a competition.

# Slalom Performance Demand Model

| Pre Event | Competition | Post Event |
|---|---|---|
| **Mastery Motivation**<br><br>Have a positive attitude to competition – see it as a challenge not a threat<br><br>Feel confident and comfortable in the race environment<br><br>Feel confident in own knowledge and experience of key technical challenges on the course, developed through quality preparation and training | **Mastery Motivation**<br><br>Be motivated to deliver best possible performance at this moment in time<br><br>Confident and positive attitude, focused on strengths not weaknesses | **Mastery Motivation**<br><br>Independently manage the immediate emotional response to the outcome, whether good or bad |
| **Decision Making**<br><br>Assess the specific technical challenges presented by the course design<br><br>Develop a plan to 'solve the problems' posed by the course designers<br><br>Remain open to late information from coaches about the course and be able to integrate into race plan | **Execution**<br><br>Focus on the here and now; the next stroke not on the race outcome<br><br>Trust in the chosen plan and own technical skills to meet the course's challenges<br><br>Be fearless and willing to take risks without 'defending a position'<br><br>Be adaptable to move to alternative tactics and paddle reactively when necessary<br><br>Maintain a steady emotional state | **Decision Making**<br><br>Rationally reflect and evaluate performance to identify learning to take into next event |
| **Teamwork**<br><br>Honest and open relationship with coach<br><br>Contribute to supportive team environment | | **Teamwork**<br><br>Honest and open relationship with coach<br><br>Contributes to supportive team environment |

And here's an example version for a sprint paddler. Clearly if you are paddling in a crew boat there is the added dimension of your communication within the boat. Decisions made during a sprint race should be tactical not technical, and ideally will be based on exercising options you've already identified in your pre-race Decision Making and planning.

# Sprint Performance Demand Model

| Pre Event | Competition | Post Event |
|---|---|---|
| **Mastery Motivation** | **Mastery Motivation** | **Mastery Motivation** |
| Have a positive attitude to competition – see racing as a challenge not a threat | Motivated to deliver best possible performance at this moment in time | Manage immediate emotional response to the outcome, whether good or bad |
| Feel confident and comfortable in the race-day environment | Confident and positive attitude, focused on strengths not my weaknesses | **Decision Making** |
| **Decision Making** | **Execution** | Rationally reflect and evaluate performance to identify learning to take forward to next heat or event |
| Can adapt race plan before the race to handle the weather conditions | Focus on executing race plan | |
| Clear and confident in ability to deliver my race plan | • First 20 strokes<br>• Maintain rhythm<br>• Go for it over last 100m | **Teamwork** |
| **Teamwork** | Focus on the here and now; next stroke not on the race outcome | Maintain honest and open relationship with coaches and support staff |
| Maintain an honest and open relationship with coaches, support staff and other paddlers in boat | Trust in physical, technical and mental capacity to execute my race plan. Only use tried and trusted simple technical cues | Contribute to a supportive team environment coaches and support staff |
| Contribute to a supportive team environment | Ready to respond to the unfolding tactical situation, but primarily want to paddle own race | |
| **1 hour pre-event** | | |
| Organize my time to ensure I warm up physically | | |
| Organize my time on and off the water to ensure mental warm up to access mastery mind-set, avoid distractions, and move into Execution | | |

Now you have your PDM, what do you do with it?

1. Rate yourself on each element. I suggest using a simple Red, Amber, Green scale.

   - Red means 'this is a consistent weakness that interferes with my performance'
   - Amber means 'this is sometimes a problem for me'
   - Green means 'this is a consistent strength'

2. Ask your coach to rate you too, then sit down together with your respective PDMs and look for differences. Remember that it's not about proving who is right or wrong, so try to be open-minded rather than defensive. Try to be curious about your different perspectives and explore them. Ask for, or provide, real examples of how you've behaved or felt in competitions to illustrate your opinions. It's a powerful exercise to do with your coach and you'll learn a lot from each other.

3. Consider whether one or more of the Fundamentals is limiting your performance or holding you back. If so, look back at the first section of this book for ideas about how to develop the Fundamentals in your regular training.

4. Review how you apply the Fundamentals after competitions and record your progress. For example, here are some notes I made about my own performance at a 'double header' slalom event:

*Mastery Motivation:*

Very good, especially after first run on race 1; confidence really clicked when I realised what I thought was mediocre was actually competitive. Race head was on, in the moment, confident. Aware of 'outcome magnet', reframed as 'I would like to win' then back to present moment. Sat in my car working on laptop between runs.

*Execution:*

As above, very good for runs 2, 3, 4. Hardly any distractions or evaluative thoughts while racing, quiet mind but determined. Not frustrated by errors; each run felt like a separate performance.

*Decision Making:*

OK. Missed impact of dropping water level on 15-17 sequence; got to take the time to look at course more closely. Did this before run 4.

*Teamwork:*

Good banter with Chris and Mike. Accommodation good, shared bunkhouse with Neal and crew.

# Race plans – Applying the Fundamentals on Race Day

You might be thinking that this all sounds very complicated because you know from experience that you need to keep things simple, especially on race day. So it's important to stress that developing a PDM for your event is different from a race day plan – although the work you do with your PDM can help you develop a more effective race plan.

A race plan is a simple checklist, a set of routines that you know will help you navigate the challenges of your event. It helps you stay focused on the process of competition rather than the outcomes.

Throughout a competition season you should aim to hone your race plan so that you become very confident in it, and trust that it will help you be well prepared, well fed and watered, and ready to perform when you need to. If your event is influenced by weather or water conditions, your plan needs to take these factors into account – for example what you will do if the wind picks up during an ocean race. Some paddlers resist developing a detailed plan because they feel it restricts them too much and they prefer to stay flexible. My counter to this is that it simply means that the plan is to stay flexible!

*Sportscene / R van Bommel*

Typically, a race plan will help you think through when you want to wake up, what and when you eat, how and when you will travel to your venue, how you will prepare for your event (eg walking a slalom course) and warm up, when you want to be on the water and for how long before you get to the start line. It will include when you meet your coach, both before and after you compete, and the timings for video review, post race nutrition or physiotherapy or massage treatment.

Whether your race plan is no more than a couple of items or a more elaborate plan, check it against the following 5 questions:

1. Does your plan keep you focused on what's important for you?
2. Is it simple?
3. Is it robust? This means that it's adaptable when stuff happens that you're not expecting.
4. Is it tried and tested so that you trust it?
5. Have you told your coach (or anyone else relevant) about what you need them to do as part of your plan?

# The key transitions

When you start thinking about your event as a series of cycles through pre-race, competition and post-race stages, you'll realise that the movement between these stages is really important. I call these *transitions*, and there are two that are particularly critical. The first is when you move from your 'ordinary life' into preparing for your event. The second is when you are on the start-line, about to transition into competition itself.

Let's look at each in more detail.

# The importance of a mental warm up

Every competitor knows that it's necessary to physically warm-up before a race. But how many pay as much attention to their mental warm-up as they do to stretching their body, loosening their muscles and increasing their heart rate? The best racers have a consistent routine that prepares body AND mind for the challenge ahead. And they practise this routine during training sessions, not just on race day.

Here are some ideas that will help you develop your own mental warm–up routine.

## 1. Deal with distractions

It's hard to race when your mind is full of the normal tasks and concerns of daily life. I remember one paddler complaining that he was thinking about the shopping list while doing full-length slalom runs! So before a race or training session give yourself the time to deal with any distractions and put them to one side. A simple technique is to write a 'to do' list, getting everything out of your head and onto a piece of paper. Then put the list away somewhere safe with a promise to return to it after the session.

## 2. Be clear about your intent

Give yourself time to sit quietly, relax and visualise what you want to achieve from the race or training session. The clearer you are about your intent, the more likely you are to achieve it. And if you can see, feel, and hear yourself performing the way you want before you start, so much the better.

> *"I was thinking about the race and how I was going to race it. Stay to my race plan, not getting distracted by the other athletes. I also remember telling myself that this race is what I've been waiting for, time to find out how good I really am."*

**Eirik Verås Larsen, 2012 K1 1000m Olympic champion**[27]

## 3. Understand the transition to your competitive mind

This is also a good time to notice your own thoughts and feelings. Competing strongly means that you are tapping into your Mastery Motivation, aspiring to be strong and focusing your energy on being in control. This is like a warrior going into battle – remember the athlete I mentioned earlier who used to mentally 'put on a suit of armour' before he competed. This focused state of mind is ideal for competition or training but it can be unproductive in your normal life, when it is often necessary to be considerate and kind to other people. In fact people who are too extreme in their Mastery Motivation in normal life can come across as insensitive or even ruthless.

So your warm-up routine helps you *transition* to a mastery state of mind. Team sports players call this 'putting their game face on'. Although this is easy for some people, others will need to take some time to tune out of normal social interactions, remind themselves of what it feels like to paddle hard and why the race or training session is important. This is particularly important to get yourself ready for the pain of competing to your maximum. You need to be ready to be tough with yourself, the course and your competitors.

Remind yourself of your different sources of self-confidence – these typically include high quality training, having good equipment, trusting your coach, and knowing from experience that you can deliver. Imagery can help too. Get creative and experiment with different mental images of yourself feeling strong and confident.

## 4.  Mentally warm-down too

After a race or training session you need to transition back to normal life. This is the reverse of warming up – you need to use your Decision Making skills to review your performance and whether or not you achieved your goals, so you can take the lessons forward to the next event. If it's been a big event, it's likely that you'll feel strong emotions – either joy or disappointment. Emotions are natural and it's important to acknowledge them before you return to your 'to do' list and take some practical steps to keep your life in order. And you can reverse from a Mastery Motivation to a more open state of mind, in which you no longer need to be so tough with yourself and other people.

# On the start line

*"Nerves? Of course I was nervous, that's when you know it means something to you! When starting with the best of the best in marathon racing at the World Champs I would say it's a combination of nerves and excitement, knowing that all your training will soon be put to the test."*

**Hank McGregor, 2011 Marathon K1 world champion**[28]

Feeling nervous before a race is natural. It's your body's response to a dangerous situation. The danger comes from a risk to self-esteem ("what if I mess up in front of everyone") or from the physical risk ("what if I get my lines wrong?"). But why is it that nerves sometimes interfere with a good performance, and at other times they help us?

For a start, it's important to acknowledge that psychologists actually don't agree on a common definition of what pre-race nerves really are. Some talk about stress, or cognitive and somatic anxiety, others about arousal and activation. I'm not sure this matters too much, because the most important factor that influences performance is your level of **confidence.**

When you are *confident* then you are far more likely to experience pre-event 'nerves' in a productive way. Some psychologists call this positive state of mind a 'challenge' mindset, and it leads to useful physiological responses that increase your heart's efficiency and energise your muscles for action. In this state of mind, you look forward to the task ahead and want to engage in it.

When you are less confident, then it's more likely that you will experience a 'threat' mindset. There are subtle but important differences in the physiological responses that lead to your body being more stressed, your heart to be less efficient and your muscles less energised. In extreme cases this is the 'dead possum' response, when you feel sleepy or lethargic. You want to avoid the race, or at least get it over and done with. If you feel a strong sense of relief after the race, it's likely that you've been in a threat mindset.[29] Movement between these two states of mind can be very fast. The fear at the top of a waterfall turns into exhilaration at the bottom, or a positive vibe can be jarred by an error in a slalom run.

What can you do to enhance your confidence and increase the chances that you'll experience a positive 'challenge' mindset when you're on the start-line?

Three of the Fundamentals are particularly important and you can influence them all:

- Your goals and motivation
- Your decision making and race plan
- The people around you

*Mastery Motivation and Goals*

Paddlers who have realistic but challenging goals will feel more confident that they can achieve them. If your goals are too stretching or unrealistic, the gap between reality and aspiration is easily filled with worry. Ideally, you will seek to achieve in a competition only what you have already proved you can do in training. Your goal in competition is simply to paddle to your level of ability. On the start-line, it helps to focus more on process goals rather than outcomes that lie in the future. Bring your attention to your immediate environment, feel your paddle, the movement of the water, and imagine your first couple of strokes. Be as present as possible and appreciate being 'right here, right now', ready and able to race.

*Decision Making*

You will be more confident when you have prepared well and have a clear plan of action that you know you can execute. You need to feel comfortable with the level of risk you are taking, because there are often choices between 'slower and safer' and 'faster and riskier'. Taking too little risk can be as damaging as taking too much. Ideally you will have developed your mental rehearsal skills so that you have tested out options in your imagination and settled on a plan that you know you can deliver. Confidence is sapped by uncertainty, so work with your coach to refine your race day routine to get you on to the start line with a clear plan.

*Other people*

It's easy to pick up, even subconsciously, on other people's fears. Make sure your race day routine only brings you into contact with people who are (realistically) positive and supportive. Remember that a competitive environment can affect how other people behave too, so you may need to avoid friends and family who you might normally spend time with. Try to avoid discussing your race with anyone who might make you question your abilities. Of course a good coach will challenge you to improve and give tough feedback, but this generally needs to happen when you can do something about it, not on race day.

Finally, remember that ultimately it matters less how you *feel* before the race than what you choose to *do* once you are on the start line. There are plenty of examples of paddlers producing great runs despite feeling sick with worry beforehand. The key is to be totally committed to your plan and do your best to deliver your own performance. Trust that once you start paddling your mindset will switch into Execution mode, the anxiety will switch to positive energy and you'll do what you have trained so hard to do.

*"I didn't look over, I don't look over once, ten metres before the finish line I wasn't positive I was winning. I just stuck to my race plan. If I came fourth with my race plan I'm worth fourth, if I come first I come first, let's just see what I can do. I didn't want to look over and see someone close and gaining so I just kept my head down and stuck to my technique."*

**Adam van Koeverden, 2012 World Champion K1 1000m[30]**

# The Olympics

*"There is no point going round and looking at the fancy lights and everything like that, at the end of the day you are there to do a job. The Olympics you will always remember, you will never forget what you do, and if you walk away from the field at the Olympics thinking I didn't give it my all or I didn't do something, you will always regret it for the rest of your life."*

**Robin Bell, 2008 Olympic Bronze medallist C1 Slalom[31]**

Only a tiny proportion of slalom or sprint athletes will ever compete at the Olympic Games. For those who do, it may well represent the pinnacle of their careers, despite the fact that it's harder to win a world championship because the field is bigger. I want to talk about some of the challenges that first time Olympians face – and offer some reminders for those who have competed at the Games before. A simple way of understanding the Olympics is to ask "what's the same, and what's different, at the Games compared to a World Championship?". The athletes who get this question right are more likely to perform to their potential.

The closer you get to being on the water for your event the more similar the Olympics are to any other big race. In fact, when it comes to your core approach and process goals, it should be no different. In slalom, it's all about the water and the poles. In sprint, the lanes will stretch out in front of you like they always do. So, successful athletes will use their regular race-day plan that they have practised and refined through the season. It's a sign of inexperience to believe that you have to do something different or special on the water just because it's the Olympics. Just the opposite – doing the basics under pressure better than anyone else will lead to a great performance.

The Olympics become more different from a World Champs the further away you get from the water. There's more security and less freedom of movement around the venue. So places that you may have been able to access during training can become inaccessible during competition. All teams will have limits on the number of accredited staff, so you will probably have fewer people on the bank than normal. The crowds will be bigger – much bigger – than at any World Championships. And they will be noisy, creating a wall of sound unlike anything you've heard before. There will be volunteers everywhere, offering to carry your boat or to give you a drink of water.

As an Olympian you are now of interest to the media, so get used to cameras and microphones in your face and manage the timing and amount of exposure. Media attention can be really useful to help build your own profile and that of your sport, so don't shy away from it. But it is wise to plan when and how you engage and respond to requests for interviews. Experienced paddlers and their teams will often make a deal with the press to do one major media conference about a week before your event on the understanding that they won't try to talk to you again until after your event. Let that event go on as long as the press wants it to and try to answer all their questions. But remember that on the days of competition you will have to pass through the 'mixed zone' when you get off the water. No matter what you've agreed with the media beforehand, there will be people with cameras and microphones asking for comments at the end of your race.

Most teams, especially from smaller nations, will stay at the Olympic Village. If you're based here you'll be living and eating in apartment blocks alongside 14,000 other people – this is a busy, vibrant and potentially distracting environment. Travel to race venues will be limited to official vehicles and buses, so you'd better get used to having less freedom of movement than you're used to. Teams with enough money will often choose to stay in their own accommodation outside the Olympic Village, because this allows them to maintain a more familiar and controllable environment. If you're staying in your own accommodation it can be fun to go and stay in the Village after your event, to soak up the atmosphere and take part in the closing ceremony.

*Sportscene / R van Bommel*

All these differences require careful planning and preparation on your part. You need to adapt and change your normal routines when you're in the Olympic environment otherwise you will find yourself out of control, either swept along by the hype or hamstrung by the security. Make sure you give yourself enough time for transit between the Village and your venue, always remember your accreditation pass, be patient with queues, and eat only what you need in the dining halls.

Preparing for the similarities and differences at the Olympics is a useful discussion to have with your coach and team-mates. It will help you maintain the consistency that you need on the water, while making the necessary changes off it. If you are fortunate enough to compete at the Games, enjoy your Olympic experience and good luck!

26. http://www.sportscene.tv/whitewater/canoe-slalom/news/waoh-what-a-day-european-champ-fiona-pennie-about-her-golden-moments

27. *http://www.sportscene.tv/flatwater/canoe-sprint/news/interview-with-multiple-olympic-champion-eirik-veras-larsen*

28. *http://www.sportscene.tv/flatwater/marathon/news/mens-k1-canoe-marathon-world-champion-hank-mcgregor-propelled-into-history*

29. The model of threat and challenge states was developed by Marc Jones and his colleagues: Jones, M., Meijen, C., McCarthy, P.J. & Sheffield, D. (2009). A theory of challenge and threat states in athletes. International Review of Sport and Exercise Psychology, 2, 161-180

30. Interview with Adam Van Koeverden, *http://www.youtube.com/watch?v=bq9OGsO_uhw&feature=c4-overview-vl&list=PL90771D0D3B295BB9*

31. *http://www.sportscene.tv/whitewater/canoe-slalom/news/interview-with-olympic-routinier-robin-bell*

# Chapter 7
## Paddling whitewater

### The psychology of risk-taking

*"In my whole life I have enjoyed risky things. If you were to ask me to jump on a longboard and cruise down a huge hill, or get a dirt bike and make a jump, I would do it. But nothing about whitewater ever really made me feel that way until I read about the risk involved. I thought 'wow that is really crazy!! I wanna try.' So the next day I talked to a friend and got the gear list and bought everything... But I didn't start from a family of paddlers, at age 17 I said, 'I want to be in the river and going off the waterfalls.'"*[32]

**Kasey Fowler, whitewater kayaker.**

Why do some people enjoy the challenge of taking risks? First off, it's likely that anyone who is attracted to whitewater has a personality preference for spending time in a spontaneous, *playful* state of mind. In this state people tend to seek new experiences, not plan too far ahead, and enjoy exciting or novel activities. This contrasts with a *serious* state of mind in which people will plan ahead and prefer things to be calm and predictable. We all switch (or reverse) between these two states of mind, and the amount of time we spend in one or the other state is shaped by our personality. There is a genetic component to the degree that people actively seek out excitement, so you can thank or blame your parents!

Sven Joos

So to apply this to paddling, I've been on trips when initially people have been in the playful state and been able to enjoy the challenge, but have reversed to a serious state when things have got too tough or they've just become tired. It's the feeling of 'I've had enough and I just want to get off this river now'. Excitement is replaced by anxiety or frustration. Of course the serious state of mind is really useful when you're planning a trip when it's important to think ahead, look at contingencies and make careful choices. And there's a reversal that many paddlers are familiar with – the sudden shift from fear above a big rapid (in the serious state) to exhilaration at the bottom of the fall (having reversed to the playful state). Sometimes a whole trip can be uncomfortable, as solo kayaker Robin Scott explains:

*"On the darkest day of the year I went alone to the Nevis, to give expression to some dark feelings: fear, loneliness, exposure to cold, wind and rain. For me, part of being human is the need to recognise these negative sensations, and solo kayaking is one way to explore them. It is strange to reflect that the actual act of kayaking alone is often unpleasant, and the positive sensations come only after success."*[33]

Psychologist Michael Apter, the originator of Reversal Theory, argues that in thrill-seeking sports like whitewater paddling, you're willing to 'buy' high levels of excitement through the level of fear you are willing to tolerate. So the greater the fear at the top of the waterfall, the greater the buzz felt at the bottom. This does rely on one key factor – self-confidence. Without self-confidence you wouldn't readily put yourself into dangerous situations, and if you did would likely feel over-anxious and too focused on the possible consequences.

Self-confidence means that you can use fear productively to weigh up the risks. All being well, you push your limits enough to get the right level of reward for the level of discomfort you're willing to face. This is a highly individual process, and can fluctuate over time. When you're 'feeling it' and confident you will generally take more on, and get more reward. When you're not 'feeling it', you will generally take fewer risks, and as a result may not experience such intense positive feelings on the water.

Here's a beautiful description by Sabrina Barm of running a big fall for the first time:

*32 feet are damn high. So high, so terrifying, the first sight of the horizon line made me cry. I had read about this waterfall (on Norway's Jordalenselvi river) long before, and for even longer, I had been dreaming of running a waterfall this high or even higher. I had run an 8m high drop before, but that 10m mark seemed magic, like a door to a new dimension. What I had not foreseen was that dreams can become bigger than reality once you wanna make them real. Of course I knew that this would be something new and that I would be scared, but I thought that I somehow could overcome nerves just like I often had in some juicy rapid, not a big deal at all. But now, the moment it should become reality, I was so scared of the drop it felt like I would never be able to do it. I was exhausted after hours on the river, and when I came round the corner, all I saw was the river dropping away into nowhere.*

*A medium, but sketchy looking drop and the horizon line of the big fall after that, you couldn't even see the pool below. My first thought was "no way!". Despair. Was it all gone? Creeking and the wish to progress into the real art of it – those dreams, that had meant so much to me, was I not strong enough to live them? Tears running down my face. After a while, I thought, I could have at least a closer look at the scenery and the pool of the big drop. Thinking of a possible line. The pool was big enough to get safe if something should go wrong. Slowly, I went back to my boat, running the first drop, letting a kayaker lead the way as a safety boater just in case I'd mess it up. Then I scouted the big drop again. I sat down on the rocks, silently. I listened. To the wind, the water, to my inner self. Until I had the answer. I moved my boat out of the eddy, into the big unknown. There was the horizon line. One last check on speed and position and there I was: Flying through the air! The flight lasted only two seconds, if at all, and the impact when I hit the water in the pool was remarkable, but not horrendous. Overwhelmed by the sight when I crossed the line, I had not leaned forward far enough, my boat had overexcited a bit and so I flipped. Being exhausted, my roll didn't work, and yes, I swam. But it doesn't matter. What matters is that I listened to my inner self and could hear the voice giving me the answer. What matters is that this answer was yes and that I found the courage to believe in myself – that I took another step forward, towards living a dream.*[34]

As skill, experience and self-confidence grow, you have to pay a higher price to get the same emotional reward, which is triggered by the release of a brain chemical called dopamine. This is the same neurochemistry that's at work in drug addicts, who over time need to take more drugs to get the same effect. This explains why paddlers can become driven to take on tougher and tougher whitewater.

*I love paddling but after having been doing it for 18 years I find that the only way I feel challenged in the sport is if I'm taking huge risks. I love the risks, but it's difficult to find falls and rapids on a daily basis that give me that challenge. In all of the other sports that I do I can tell that the learning curve is still steep, and I'm constantly being challenged because there is so much more to learn.*

**Tao Berman, extreme kayaker**[35]

It's a sign of paddling maturity to safely manage the drive to take bigger and bigger risks. Sadly, it often takes a bad swim – your own or a paddling buddy's – to step out of this cycle and decide what your limits are. This happened to me after a particularly long and sticky encounter with a stopper on the River Ötz back in 1983.

*"We (a motley collection of Aussie, Kiwi and Austrian slalom paddlers) had gravitated to Landeck in Austria, paddling the Inn and its tributaries the Sanne and Ötz. Things changed forever for me after a trip on the upper reaches of the Inn. We'd paddled the same section earlier in the week, and this time we paid little attention to the fact that the water was about half a metre higher. The first main rapid is called the High Judge, and I remember passing over a big wave and dropping into a meaty hole that I couldn't recall from our earlier trip. I was relaxed at first, thinking that I'd just roll up and out of the hole. But it was one of those stoppers that don't like to let go, and after couple of rolls and getting more water than air it began to dawn on me that I was in trouble. My slalom boat must have broken, because I was tail down and still getting worked round and round. Thinking that my only hope was to swim, I let go of my paddle just as my boat, now full of water, flushed from the hole. Now I was floating down the rest of the rapid in a sunken boat with no paddle. I frantically grabbed my paddle and managed to get closer to the river bank, where I dragged myself out, exhausted, as my boat washed away. Water was still draining from my sinuses later that night."*

I suppose many paddlers have an equivalent story of a bad swim

or particularly nasty close shave.[36] Something really fundamental
changed for me after mine. Although it's a little embarrassing to
admit it now, that was the moment when I realised that I wasn't
immortal. It hit me for real that I could die doing the sport I loved.
I learned that I had to take care, inspect more, to be more alert
to the dangers. That doesn't mean I stopped taking risks, but the
experience marked a shift in my attitude to rivers and towards
myself. Up until then I felt I couldn't fail, that I could take anything
a river could throw at me. Bluntly, I was cocky and not a little
arrogant. I like to think that I developed some humility and respect
for the river that day, two qualities that I hope have served me well
both on and off the water ever since.

Jonathan Males

# Using the Fundamentals to build Self Confidence

You can think of running a river as a whole series of performances,
with each major rapid requiring preparation, execution and review.
Just as in a competition, the same psychological fundamentals of
Mastery Motivation, Decision Making and Teamwork all create self-

confidence and the ability to Execute well. Self-confidence allows you to tolerate the fear, or at best feel the excitement, at the top of a big rapid. Self-confidence also makes it possible to transition from conscious thinking into autopilot, relying on well-grooved paddling skills. If the fundamentals aren't in place you'll get stuck in 'paralysis through analysis' and are more likely to paddle poorly or make a mistake.

## Mastery Motivation

First of all, consider your motivation. Why do you want to paddle the river or the rapid in the first place? Ideally, you will want to paddle whitewater in order to test and challenge your own skill. This is a useful expression of intrinsic Mastery Motivation. Feeling overly anxious is a sign that you may be biting off more than you can chew, perhaps for the wrong reasons. You are more likely to get into trouble if you are motivated to paddle by a fear of looking weak, a desire to impress your friends, or misplaced competitiveness with your paddling mates. So stay aware of how you're thinking and feeling, particularly how you talk to yourself on the river. Are you listening to your inner critic, telling you that you're not good enough, or to your inner coach, reminding you of your ability and encouraging you to paddle well? Learn to ignore your critical thoughts and focus instead on your strengths.

## Decision Making

When you are paddling to impress others or under peer pressure you will find that your Decision Making can become skewed. High anxiety will narrow your attention and you may miss important details of a rapid or get fixated on just one feature. Over-confidence can be just as dangerous, and you may not look closely enough at the details of the rapid and ignore potential problems. Good decision making on a river is all about balancing the risk and reward. The higher the risk, the greater the emotional reward when things go well, and vice versa. So it requires a clear understanding of the risks and an accurate assessment of your own ability to paddle whitewater in the psychological sweet spot between boredom and panic. By staying true to your own abilities and seeking only to challenge yourself you're more likely to keep a clear head and make wise choices.

Decision Making is also impacted by fatigue. Towards the end of a long day you're more likely to fix on one part of a rapid and miss important details. When this has happened to me I've been caught out by features that looked easy at first glance, yet turned out to be trickier than I realised. Fatigue is also a major confidence-sapper, because once you start to get tired you're more likely to make mistakes, which in turn knocks your confidence, and so a negative spiral begins. So make sure you do enough conditioning work in the gym, or paddle regularly, so that you feel good and strong in your body. And although enjoying a few drinks is often a key ingredient in a good paddling weekend, being on a river too hung-over isn't a good look. Remember that for most of us, going out for a night's drinking is possible at any time, but to be out on a river is a special treat.

Once you're clear about your motivation, watch one or two competent people run a drop, then imagine you are running the rapid the same way. See and feel yourself taking the right strokes at the right time, getting your boat into the right places and holding your line. On a complex rapid it can also be worth considering a 'what if' scenario and rehearsing how you would deal with it. For example, if you miss your preferred channel and end up going down a different line, what would you do? If the consequences of this option are too unpleasant it might lead you to think again about your plan! Don't spend too long looking though – it rarely helps and you can get overwhelmed or stuck in your thoughts. It's also good practice on a river to keep moving downstream and avoid too much standing around getting cold.

*Deb Pinniger*

## Execution

Sitting in the eddy above a big rapid or fall is just like being on the start-line of a race. Anxiety is a sign that your attention is on the future rather than on the present moment. Catch negative thoughts early, and instead remember a time when you've paddled strongly. Remind yourself that fear is natural and that it's the price you're willing to pay for the thrill of whitewater. Bring your attention back to the present moment, inwards to your breathing, feel your paddle in your hands, tune into your boat and the movement of the water. Become focused on what you can see and feel around you. You may want to run through the lines in your imagination one final time before taking a deep breath and a strong stroke out into the current. Develop your own consistent routine for these moments above a major rapid, so that it becomes a source of familiarity and confidence.

**Teamwork**

Good teamwork helps in many ways – from feeling confident that the person holding the throw-bag knows what to do with it, to knowing who paddles at a similar level to you so that you can watch how they manage a rapid, to knowing who tends to be over- or under-confident so that you can ignore their advice! The best paddling groups are held together by mutual respect rather than being driven by individual egos. This makes them safer and more supportive of each person's individual decisions, and helps to build a sense of collective confidence.

After a major rapid, or at the end of a trip, it's time to review. There are plenty of high fives after a good line down a big rapid, but after the emotional buzz it's important to move back into a more rational Decision Making mode to learn the lessons. Many paddlers aren't rigorous about this on the river and generally it's straight on to the next rapid. The review tends to come once you're off the river and enjoying a cold beer. But maybe that's the best time for it, because it tends to build Teamwork at the same time!

**Your self confidence checklist**

*Mastery Motivation*

What is my motivation for paddling this river / rapid? Am I doing it because I really feel up for it on my own terms, or am I doing it to maintain my ego and self-esteem? Am I allowing myself to be pressured into it?

*Decision Making*

Can I see the right lines and the key paddle strokes? Have I weighed up the options and risks? Can I visualise myself paddling the lines I want to? Can I imagine myself responding to a mistake and paddling 'Plan B'?

*Execution*

Am I confident in my ability and feeling settled in my boat? Is my focus on the 'here and now'?

*Teamwork*

What is the quality of our teamwork? Are we talking constructively, testing our thinking with each other, watching each other's lines? Are we taking enough time and care to set safety?

# When it all goes wrong

A single bad experience, whether it's a nasty swim with downtime, seeing one of your mates hurt, or getting injured yourself, can shatter your confidence. It's easy to take your confidence for granted and it can come as a big shock when you lose it. The pain of an injury is a constant reminder that you made a mistake on the river, and injury can create a psychological challenge all on its own.

Here's an example from Louise Jull, a world class extreme kayaker, writing about a broken scapula she suffered in a swim on the Green River:

*"The fortunate thing about bone injuries is that they heal back to 100% in 6-8 weeks. The harder part in my mind is the fact that I let this happen, I messed up and made the mistake, which led to this accident. I should have got out of my boat and scouted the rapid again, taken it more seriously and been sure of my line. What scares me is that I messed up the other day. Something in my brain was not working or making me stop and think about what I was doing, I was*

*not sure of the line and I still went. Human error maybe but this is something I could have avoided. I know I could have because I owned that rapid just a couple of days earlier. It was not a question of could I do it or not, I had already done it well. Just mentally I was not strong and this reflected in my pathetic strokes and hesitation. My confidence in my ability is low right now and I feel super gutted. Kayaking class 4/5 requires confidence and I feel like I let myself down the other day."*[37]

Let's look at the different factors involved when you have a bad experience like this and get injured on the water.

## Injury damages your self-esteem, not just your body

A serious injury does more than hurt your body – it can also challenge your sense of identity and self-esteem. Anyone who is talented, passionate about their sport and devotes serious time and effort will feel pride in his or her achievements and skill. Kayaking becomes more than something you do; it becomes who you are. This merging of identity with activity is more prevalent with younger paddlers. They often have more time to devote to paddling and they have had less time on the planet to diversify and develop different skills and aspects of their identity. So whilst older paddlers might be more prone to getting hurt because of their ageing, battered bodies, the psychological impact may be less because they have a non-paddling career and family commitments that contribute to their sense of identity. For younger paddlers it's important to develop a sense of perspective, especially about rehabilitation time spent off the water. This can easily feel like wasted time and create frustration – which isn't good for confidence. Instead, see it as a positive opportunity to spend time with people and do things you wouldn't normally do. Like learning Spanish in preparation for your trip to Chile, or visiting your family who haven't seen you for the last six months.

*Deb Pinniger*

### Emotional turmoil

A bad experience on the river, whether combined with an injury
or not, can also lead to unproductive self-blame. You find yourself
going over the incident again and again, wishing it were different
and at the same time telling yourself how stupid / unlucky / clumsy
you were to get in that situation. It's important to reflect carefully on
an incident and take appropriate responsibility for your actions, so
you can learn and move on. But when this is also tangled up with
lots of emotions it's rarely productive. So what can you do instead?

First of all, give yourself time to acknowledge your own emotions.
Particularly after a bad swim, this can take some time to work
through. It's often not easy to face strong emotions like fear or anger.
And sometimes there's a reluctance to do so, because whitewater
paddlers are 'supposed' to be tough, ice-cool in the face of danger,
and always ready to get back in their boat and charge down the
river. But the reality of suffering a bad injury or having a near death
experience is not like that. Remember that emotions are short-lived
physiological responses, so if an emotion is lasting many hours
after an event, the chances are that you are doing something in your
head to keep it going. Naming and expressing emotions helps you
to process them and move on. Write it down, tell someone, or just

say out loud what you're feeling, without defending or justifying yourself.

**Learning from experience**

Only once you have reached some level of emotional equilibrium, can you start to reflect more objectively and learn from your experience. It's important to get the right balance when looking for reasons why things have gone wrong. Some causes will be down to you – so you need to 'look in the mirror'. And it's also likely that some causes will be due to other people's actions or inactions, environmental factors or equipment – so you also need to 'look out the window'. Focus only on the internal factors and you can endlessly beat yourself up and never regain confidence. Focus only on external causes and you may feel better, but you may also miss important learning about yourself. The key is to identify what you can control yourself and do differently next time. By being objective and thorough it's easier to draw a line under your analysis and move on. The self-confidence checklist shown earlier gives some useful questions to help you review and learn from your experience.

# Rebuilding your confidence

Confidence is built up over time from many sources. If you've lost confidence after an accident or injury here's how to systematically rebuild your confidence:

*Re-kindle your Mastery Motivation*

Remind yourself why you love paddling so much, think about the great times you've had and your favourite trips. If you can, watch video of yourself paddling well. If you find that you're still mentally beating yourself up about what happened, replace your inner critic with an inner coach. Don't tell yourself anything you wouldn't want to hear from someone else. Practise mindfulness to help settle your mind and find your emotional equilibrium.

*Use the power of your imagination*

There's so much quality video available now, especially from head-mounted Go-Pro cameras that it's possible to see what it's like to run most rivers. Don't just watch in awe; instead *imagine* yourself into the scene so you can see, hear and feel yourself paddling well. Don't spend time watching carnage clips or lots of less competent paddlers – this will just sap your confidence or remind you of your own bad experience. When you're ready, in your imagination replay the incident where you were hurt or messed up, but nail the lines and paddle the rapid successfully. Keep doing this till your inner experience is consistently positive and realistic.

*Feel the love*

It's possible your self-esteem has taken a battering too, so hang out with people you like and who like you. And not just your paddling buddies; remember you can get strength and affirmation from non-paddling friends and family. The important thing is to spend time with people who love and appreciate you for who you are – not just your paddling skill!

*Connect with nature*

Even if you can't paddle because of injury, spend time doing fun things outdoors. We are so fortunate as paddlers to spend time on beautiful rivers, lakes or the ocean in fantastic parts of the world. It's important to stay connected with nature, even if it means walking or cycling rather than paddling.

Deb Pinniger

*Build up gradually*

Once you start paddling again, build up gradually. You don't need
to go right back to the beginning, but don't expect to start where
you left off, either. Make sure that you paddle with people you like
and feel confident with, and focus on enjoying the whole paddling
experience – not just the stout stuff.

## Conclusion

This chapter has explored the psychology of risk-taking as it applies to whitewater kayaking. I've shown how the four Fundamentals come together to create the self-confidence that allows you to buy excitement with your willingness to feel fear. The principles are exactly the same if you're heading out into big surf on a SUP or contemplating a tricky open sea crossing, or indeed in any situation where you need to perform under pressure.

*Deb Pinniger*

---

32. *http://www.teamdagger.com/profiles/blogs/welcome-to-whitewater*

33. *http://worldkayakblogs.com/robinsolos/* Nevis 31 Dec 13

34. *http://www.sportscene.tv/whitewater/extreme/news/my-first-flight*

35. *http://playak.com/article.php?id=11060*

36. For a powerful essay exploring mortality on the river, read *http://www.sitezed.com/life-and-death-beyond-the-edge/*

37. *http://www.sportscene.tv/whitewater/extreme/news/human-error-gorilla-by-louise-jull*

# Chapter 8
## Women on the water

### Meet Bill

AEphotos.co.uk / A Edmonds

The inspiration for this chapter came from a short conversation I had with an unknown kayaker one wet, wintery Saturday by the River Dart. After an exhilarating run down the upper Dart, I gave a lift to a 'Bill', a guy hitchhiking back up the hill to collect his car. We started talking, and he was clearly disturbed by his last 4 hours on the river. (For those unfamiliar with the Upper Dart, it's a classic Grade 3-4 + run, and at this day's level an experienced group can blast down in less than an hour). "Women!" he exclaimed. I was reminded of Norm from the TV show Cheers grumbling, "Women – you can't live with them. Pass the beer-nuts". My new companion had just paddled the river with a small group that included 'Sue' his girlfriend, and it became apparent that she hadn't enjoyed the trip very much. As a result, neither had he. "She was just crying – she wouldn't bloody paddle," he complained. "I just don't understand her!" I mentioned that I was a sport psychologist, and Bill said, "Well I'd really like to know how you're supposed to paddle with women." I never had the chance to talk to Bill's girlfriend to find out what she thought about the trip, but his questions started me thinking about the psychology of women and canoeing. This is clearly a risky topic for a male writer, so I asked a few of my women paddling friends for their views and explored some of the research on gender differences.

# What women paddlers say

My women friends, a combination of slalom paddlers, wildwater racers and recreational river paddlers from four different countries, told me that they were attracted to the sport by their sense of adventure and because canoeing looked fun. Each quickly became hooked by the challenge of mastering the sport and they liked the sense of identity that came with being a canoeist. All mentioned the importance of a dynamic river environment, in terms of appreciating the fast glide of a kayak on whitewater or the opportunity to find a sense of peace in wild places. As women they reported few barriers to participating in canoeing, although one noted that race prizes were rarely equivalent for men's and women's events, and all were frustrated by the gender imbalance in the Olympic disciplines. They all sought to overcome a relative lack of strength by becoming more skillful than the men. But there wasn't a strong sense of discrimination; in fact Andrea said, *"Paddling is actually the place where I feel most free of gender barriers. In paddling, I always feel accepted for who I am and what I am able to contribute. In paddling I am able to express who I am and I'm accepted for that. Maybe it's because whitewater paddling demands social equity as everyone is looking after each other and anyone can end up in trouble. Maybe it's because of the non-conformist thinking of paddlers. Whatever it is, I love it."*

They welcomed the growth in female paddling groups around the world. Not because they didn't enjoy paddling with men - *"the social aspect and being surrounded by driven people who love the same sport is also a very enjoyable aspect"* – but because they experienced a different dynamic: *"paddling with other competent women paddlers is such a joy! Perhaps it's the like-mindedness of paddling with people who know of fear and juggling commitments, of not conforming to societal norms and just doing what you love."*

As US paddler and writer Ky Delaney says about the merits of women paddling with women:

*"Paddling with all-women groups has also helped to develop my ability to look after people on the water. I used to assume that the guys on a kayak trip will chase down a swimmer and boat. But when I'm paddling with all women, I take a more active role in helping to resolve any mishaps. Paddling with other women also means taking turns getting out front. Leading through the rapids plays a huge role in developing water-reading skills. As scary as it might feel for your girlfriend to be out in front, she'll love the unobstructed view. It'll feel like it's just her and the water. Besides, other women push each other. Women on the water have encouraged me in ways that a significant other never could have. When I see a female friend dominate a wave or nail a line, I am inspired that I can do the same. Female paddlers are often more comparable to me in terms of body size and strength. When I see that they can make a certain move, I often believe more in my own ability to pull off the same move. When I hear a woman shout, "you got it," I somehow believe it at a different level. Women laugh and chat more. While guys tend to brag about their kayaking resumes and tell epic stories, we women tend to swap tales about our personal lives. I have decided to date a guy, quit jobs, buy houses, move across the country, and take other risks while paddling with my favourite lady paddlers. I've also ended several paddles with sore abs not from the paddling, but from laughing so hard."[38]*

# What the research says about gender differences

AEphotos.co.uk / A Edmonds

So although my sample of women paddlers isn't big enough to be a valid statistical sample, we can speculate that successful women canoeists are attracted to canoeing, and get satisfaction from it, because they like mastering its challenge, they appreciate the natural environment, and they enjoy hanging out with other paddlers. Perhaps not a very different list of reasons than you'd find from *any* paddler, male or female. Yet there are differences in aspects of men and women's psychology. The academic research suggests that women tend to be more risk averse than men[39], and are less likely to be attracted to high-risk 'adrenaline' sports than men[40]. Men and women approach risk differently too. When weighing up whether to run a big rapid, a 'typical' male response is to be highly motivated by the possibility of success – the positive buzz, a boost to reputation, a great photo – and not overly concerned by the risk of taking a swim. The equation only starts to shift if there is a real danger of serious injury or death. A typical female response is to see the risk of a swim first and once acknowledged, this tends to outweigh any positive benefits of paddling the rapid successfully. Women also tend to be less confident in their ability than men, regardless of the reality of their skill. Perhaps as a result, the death rate for young men from accidents and misadventure is higher than that of young women, so there are some downsides to male over-confidence too! [41] There are also gender differences in attitudes towards competition, with men more likely than women to seek out individual and team competitive opportunities, and to more highly value asserting their physical strength. Men will tend to value mastery over caring; women will tend to value caring over mastery.

Findings like these are based on the questionnaire responses of large numbers of people and they can obscure individual differences, so of course there are women who are quite willing to take risks and to compete, just as there are men who are very cautious and prefer to co-operate. And at a really high level, female athletes can be just as competitive as the men. So these are group trends, not blanket descriptions of all men and women. Individual personality will play a role in what activities people are attracted to and what they persevere with. People with a personality wired to take more risks and a preference for excitement will tend to enjoy canoeing more than those who prefer less risk. Assuming equal opportunities exists, it's fair to argue that people will self select into and out of canoeing – regardless of whether they are male or female. There will be people of either gender who are hooked despite finding aspects of the sport difficult or unpleasant. As Laura said, *"Despite not liking the cold the first week, something made me want to go back,"* and Luuka reported, *"I didn't like paddling when I initially started as it threw me out of my comfort zone. I didn't enjoy learning to Eskimo roll or the thought of being trapped upside down in a kayak".* In both these cases the paddlers persevered, driven by their motivation to master the challenge – as Laura said, *"I also got a lot of satisfaction from overcoming challenges that came as part of training and racing".*

Most paddlers need encouragement and nurture early on in their paddling careers. And it's likely that men and women need different types of support. There is research evidence that male and female athletes have different needs of their coaches, with male athletes primarily valuing a coach's technical expertise, while female athletes most value a coach's ability to provide a supportive relationship[42]. As Laura explained, *"As you move up through the sport it is good to have the support from someone close to you that can offer support and a logical voice. This does not necessarily need to be a coach or someone knowledgeable about the sport particularly, just someone who you trust and can be open with."* If we extrapolate this finding, it suggests that when the going gets tough at the top of a rapid, male paddlers may first need to hear a competent voice explaining what to do, and then only rarely want reassurance. Female paddlers may prefer to hear emotional reassurance first, and then listen to instructions about the right line to take.

# Some questions for Bill and Sue

So let's take an imaginary return to the Upper Dart, as Bill and his Sue make their way downstream. What is Sue's motivation for going canoeing on that cold, wet winter's day? Is she attracted by the challenge of mastering a demanding set of skills, does it look fun, and does she like an outdoors environment? Or is she perhaps going paddling today because this is the only way of spending weekend time with Bill? Group dynamics often get complicated when there's a personal relationship involved, whether that's a parent –child, sibling or romantic partner. These types of relationships are typically far more intense than normal friendships because of the emotional history and mutual expectations. I wonder how much of Bill's frustration comes from the fact that Sue is a woman, and how much comes from the fact she is his girlfriend? And vice versa – how much of Sue's upset comes from the fact that it's her boyfriend seeing her cold, wet and scared?

Does Bill appreciate Sue's different appetite for taking risks? Does he realise that she is probably looking at a rapid and seeing everything that could go wrong, while he just sees the line and the big eddy at the bottom? Does he appreciate that she might not be ready to 'just bloody paddle' until she's been reassured and helped to feel safe?

Intriguing questions, and the sort of questions I'd encourage Bill, Sue and the rest of us to bear in mind. They might help answer his original question about paddling with women.

# The Fundamentals – likely differences between men and women

### Mastery Motivation

This is important for all paddlers, men and women. Fewer women will express competitiveness and a desire for control than men, but both men and women can and do strive for high standards.

### Execution

No evidence of gender differences.

### Decision Making

Men and women tend to assess risk differently. Men will tend to put a higher value on the positive outcomes and pay less attention to the possible downsides of an activity – unless there are really serious consequences. Women tend to be put off from taking part in an activity if there is *any* risk of harm, and will not easily be swayed by possible positive outcomes. Men tend to be more confident of success than women (even when this is not true).

### Teamwork

Women are more likely to seek, and provide, emotional support to each other. Men are more likely to seek, and provide, expertise to each other. Despite this, everyone needs both – shared expertise and support.

38. *http://www.blueridgeoutdoors.com/paddling/how-to-not-kayak-with-your-girlfriend/*

39. Gender differences in risk taking: A meta-analysis. By Byrnes, James P.; Miller, David C.; Schafer, William D. Psychological Bulletin, Vol 125(3), May 1999, 367-383

40. *http://www.ncbi.nlm.nih.gov/pmc/articles/PMC3757272/*

41. *http://journal.sjdm.org/06016/jdm06016.htm*

42. Hays, K., Maynard, I., Thomas, O., & Bawden, M. (2007). Sources and types of confidence identified by world class sport performers. Journal of Applied Sport Psychology, 19, 434-456

# Chapter 9
## Paddling with Young People

Deb Pinniger

## Learning to be a paddling parent

Becoming a parent usually means it's time to renegotiate the role of paddling in your life. Of course there are those with incredibly supportive partners, living right next to a river, who can keep on boating uninterrupted after the arrival of a youngster. But for most of us, it means a pretty significant reduction in opportunities to go paddling. This can be tough to accept, but most parents find that the loss of paddling time soon becomes a minor issue compared to the challenges of disturbed sleep, dirty nappies and colic. And you may even find that being a parent is so much fun too, especially as children grow, that you're happy to give up some paddling time.

One psychological change that many paddlers notice once they become a parent is that they start to re-calibrate the level of risk they are prepared to take. Knowing that you are responsible for another human being usually makes the negative consequences of messing up a big rapid feel a lot more significant.

Peter Kauzer, Slalom K1 world champion on becoming a father:

*"I am extremely happy that my lifelong wish became true – I am a father. Once you hold your baby for the first time, you forget about everything else, all the bad and good things that happened before become irrelevant. Once Nola was born everything now revolves around her. She makes my days shorter, she makes me happy and because of her I wake up with a smile. It is hard for me to go to training and leave my daughter. Before her birth I always went for a coffee after training or had a talk with someone, but now I go straight home... Now I wake up a bit earlier than before, although Nola sleeps well. When I return from training I cannot lie down on a couch, relax and do nothing, I have to occupy myself with my daughter. She is a very happy child, she smiles a lot. Every day brings something new. The only thing is, you get tired sooner in the evening, so you go to bed earlier than before. Janja is understanding, so we divide everything and I can maintain my normal training regime."*[43]

At some stage you'll probably want to introduce your offspring to your chosen paddling discipline. I've always been wary of pushing my children too hard, having seen too many examples over the years of kids who have ended up living out their parents' unfulfilled aspirations – usually with disastrous consequences. I remember meeting one boy who burned out at the age of 13 after a couple of years' hard slalom training being 'coached' by his demanding father. The poor lad never paddled again and hated canoeing.

Thankfully there are also many examples of children successfully following their parents into the sport and finding fulfillment in the process. The parents who get it right make paddling fun and encourage their kids to make friends and enjoy the social side of the sport. They don't put too much pressure on their children, and let them make their own choices about taking part. They remain encouraging and supportive regardless of competitive results, and make sure their kids learn how to paddle safely and make good decisions on the river.

*AEphotos.co.uk / A Edmonds*

Once your children develop to the stage of being active competitors, you will face a whole new set of challenges as a paddling parent. First up is navigating your relationship with coaches and team officials. From the age of 15 or so, many youngsters prefer to listen to instruction and feedback from a coach rather than a parent. So make sure you understand when your child becomes the responsibility of a team and when you need to manage them yourself. Resist the temptation to interfere with the coach's decisions and take a back seat at events unless the coach has given you a job. During a competition, be aware that some paddlers don't like their parents watching so accept this and watch from a discreet distance. If your child likes you to be there (and most do), make sure they know where you will be. They may not make eye contact but they will see you. Keep smiling, even if their race doesn't go to plan because the last thing they need is a glum face watching on. Remember who is there to race – there is a very fine line between encouragement and trying to achieve through your child. Take great care not to cross it. If you haven't seen your child in a competitive environment before, remember that their demeanour and mood may be different from normal. They may be more intense, moody or less friendly than you expect. Give them space and stay positive.[44]

# Laying the right foundations

Whether you're a parent, a coach, youth leader or professional instructor, you can help young paddlers to get extra benefits from paddling by also ensuring that they lay down the foundations for the four Fundamentals. These mental strengths will help them whatever they do later in life, whether or not that includes pursuing a serious competitive career in sport. I believe that the real gift of sport is the opportunity to develop life-long skills and attitudes, because success in life usually depends on self-discipline and it's important that people learn this early in life. The Fundamentals are all forms of self-discipline. Paddle–sports are particularly powerful because they take place in dynamic, natural environments that bring an extra level of challenge, complexity and beauty. Here are some considerations about each of the four Fundamentals for young paddlers.

**Mastery Motivation: Help young paddlers set high standards for themselves**

Young people may rarely admit it, but parents and other adults are powerful role models especially when it comes to shaping their motivation. This happens particularly through parents' spoken and unspoken expectations and how they respond to young people's efforts and performances. The behaviour you reinforce and reward is the behaviour that your child will repeat. If they come to believe that your attention and love for them are linked to their competitive results, they will strive to achieve great results. The dark side of this behaviour is that your child's self-esteem will become closely linked with their sporting success – fine when they're doing well, but disastrous when they fail because they will perceive a poor performance as a blow to their very identity and self-esteem. They will struggle to be resilient in the face of setbacks and won't develop a solid base for a healthy, robust personality.

Of course it's appropriate to be proud and supportive when your child wins a race, but it's far more important to reward and reinforce the quality of their effort, their determination and their competitive attitude. Teach them to set high standards for themselves and to aspire to mastery over themselves and the river, not simply to try to beat the other competitors. They need to know that your love and encouragement are unconditional, not based on their success as a paddler. This will give them a sound foundation for Mastery Motivation and self-confidence that will sustain them through their lives.

**Decision Making: Help young paddlers learn how to plan and think ahead.**

Children and teenagers are not generally very good at thinking ahead. Children under the age of about 10 are unable to think about abstract ideas, so won't be able to assess risks that aren't immediately obvious. So you'll need to teach them what to do in a very clear and pragmatic way. As they get older they will develop more capacity to think conceptually, but there is growing evidence that teenagers' capacity to plan ahead actually gets worse for a while as their brains mature and 're-wire' into adulthood. Let's take a short diversion into neuroscience to understand why this is. The frontal lobes of their brain are responsible for inhibiting strong emotions and impulsive thoughts. They provide the voice of reason that considers the likely consequence of an action that allows us to choose what to do, rather than react impulsively. Alcohol takes this part of the brain out of action, which is why people behave so differently when they are drunk; the brakes come off, and the impulses are let loose! The frontal lobes are not well developed and are still growing in the teenage brains. Combine this with the massive hormonal changes that take place through puberty, and you can start to see why teenagers are so often unpredictable, impulsive and seemingly incapable of thinking about the consequences of their actions.[45] It's a bit like they're drunk all the time.

What does this mean if you're coaching or parenting teenagers? For a start, don't try to argue with biology. Accept that a teenager will not necessarily plan ahead very far or very well. Their time horizon will be about 30 minutes into the future – even less for boys. They are not behaving like this to annoy you or because they are stupid. It's just how it is.

Fortunately you can help them (and their brains) by taking a coaching approach. Ask good questions that help them to identify options, size up risks, and consider possible outcomes. This will help them take on the risks and challenges of paddle sports more safely. Of course you can just tell them what to do, but how many teenagers are going to listen? By questioning rather than telling, you'll help their brains mature faster because they have to think through their options and the consequences themselves.

**Execution: Help young paddlers learn how to focus**

In this wired world teenagers (and the rest of us) face constant demands on attention. It's all too easy to get into a reactive, hyper-vigilant state of mind where we're multi-tasking and constantly waiting for the latest tweet or Facebook update. The upside is a sense of connection, but the downside is that few people are ever fully present and paying attention to the task at hand. What sort of a problem this creates is a matter of some debate amongst psychologists and neuroscientists. Some argue that a wired world is leading to changes in brain function and reduced empathy in young people, where others take a more positive view on the benefits of the Internet[46]. Whatever the real impact, paddling takes young people away from smart-phone screens, and the challenges of mastering whitewater, surfing an ocean swell or learning to balance a sprint kayak, all demand sustained attention of a different order than modern daily life. Add in the increased challenges of a competitive environment and paddle sports offer a fantastic opportunity for young people to develop their capacity to sustain their focus on their bodies and the physical world around them.

Teach them to increase their self-awareness and pay attention to their body as they paddle. Encourage their respect of the river environment, to look around them and appreciate the natural world. Teach them to closely watch the patterns of moving water and understand its forces. Encourage them to view competition as a chance to learn how to discipline themselves and learn how to focus their energy and attention.

**Teamwork: Help young paddlers learn how to treat others with respect**

Paddling, especially on whitewater or the sea, provides brilliant opportunities for young people to develop the skills and attitudes that underpin Teamwork. Paddling together in a challenging environment requires collaboration, giving and receiving support, communication and mutual respect. Learning to rely on a friend with a throw-bag builds mutual trust. Seeing how people respond to challenging situations helps young people to recognise and appreciate personality differences. And young people can also bully, intimidate and be casually cruel to each other – remember the savagery of the children in 'Lord of the Flies'? If you're in the position of being a responsible adult, it's your responsibility to set the standards for inter-personal behaviour and mutual respect. It will be up to you to 'call' unacceptable behaviour like bullying.

Be aware of the risk of letting this role slip in a desire to be liked or appear cool to your younger companions. You won't be doing anyone a favour if you do so.

---

43. http://www.sportscene.tv/whitewater/canoe-slalom/news/peter-kauzer-looks-back-on-his-highs-and-lows-in-2012

44. Tim Ward contributed many of the practical tips on parenting a competitive paddler – thanks Tim!

45. http://www.nimh.nih.gov/health/publications/the-teen-brain-still-under-construction

46. https://theconversation.com/your-brain-on-the-internet-a-response-to-susan-greenfield-8694

# Chapter 10
## Canoeing through life

*"You don't stop canoeing because you get old,*
*you get old because you stop canoeing"*

**– Bumper sticker spotted by a river.**

Since I first stepped into a kayak at the age of 12, paddling has been a major theme in my life. At times it was absolutely central, especially from my late teens and twenties when I was pretty much a full-time slalom paddler. I then spent many hours standing on often cold and windy riverbanks holding a stopwatch or video camera as a coach, and my own paddling took a back seat. Paddling stayed in the background while my children were young, but over the last ten years I've re-engaged in the sport, as a paddling parent, whitewater kayaker and slalom racer. Nearly 40 years' involvement in the sport has given me an interesting perspective and raised my curiosity about the role canoeing has through life, and how we engage with it differently as we age. This chapter is intended to help you understand some of life's key transitions and how they might relate to your paddling career.

## Physical changes

Ageing causes obvious physical changes that affect paddling. Your heart's maximal rate declines with age, and $VO_2$ max, a measure of your maximum ability to take in and use oxygen, normally declines by about 1% per year after the mid twenties. In men, the level of the hormone testosterone drops from the early twenties, contributing to reduced muscle mass and muscle glycogen levels. Eyesight starts to deteriorate from the age of 40. Bones get more brittle and prone to breaking while recovery takes longer. All this means that older paddlers can't sustain the same volume and intensity of training as their younger counterparts.

Andi Uhl

If this all sounds depressing, the good news is that staying active in the right way slows down your body's natural decline with age. Paddle sports offer an ideal form of exercise; especially disciplines like whitewater, slalom, or surfing that involve short, intense bursts of effort and a dynamic range of movement. These types of paddling provide a natural form of interval training, a well-known training method in all the competitive disciplines. There is growing evidence that high intensity interval training helps the body's cells to produce short bursts of energy and is more effective at reducing the physiological impact of ageing than long, slow distance at lower intensity. The main disadvantage of intense exercise is that it is uncomfortable compared to more moderate aerobic (steady state) exercise, so it requires more motivation to sustain.

If you want to keep on paddling, as you get older, you'll need to think about some training off the water too. It's well proven that strength training helps to maintain muscle mass, which allows the muscles to work harder for longer. Weight training also helps to maintain bone density as you age, so all the more reason to get into the gym regularly[47]. Lower intensity training like Pilates or Yoga also plays an important role because it help to develop your core – the deep stabilizing muscles beneath your stomach and lower back. A strong core helps to maintain flexibility, prevents injury and eases the inevitable aches and pains of ageing.

Be sensible and take your general level of health and fitness into account before doing any exercise, on or off the water, which makes you out of breath. If in doubt, check with your doctor before drastically increasing your activity level. Whatever your style of paddling, whether you prefer a long cruise on a lake or a vigorous burst on whitewater, regular exercise of any kind leads to greater health, vitality, positive mood and mental alertness as you get older[48].

# What changes psychologically as we age – and how is this relevant for canoeists?

Psychologist Erik Ericson identified a pattern of life transitions through eight stages from early childhood through to old age[49]. Like any theory, Erikson's has its limitations but it's still a useful framework for understanding the changes in motivation and priorities that can happen over a paddler's lifetime. Erikson's theory suggests that people are faced with a key challenge or 'crisis' at each stage of life, which forces them to deal with a combination of biological (such as ageing) and sociocultural factors (such as the expectations of getting a job or starting a family). He believed that if a person successfully reconciles the crisis they face at each stage they gain a particular virtue that will serve them in later life. If they don't reconcile a stage's challenge the issue will reappear in later life – like 'unfinished business'. There is not a fixed time span for each stage and an individual's life will rarely follow the neat pattern described by the theory.

Erikson's model began with birth, but we'll pick it up from the fifth stage, adolescence, given that this is the age at which many people start to get involved in canoe sport and really take it seriously.

## Adolescence: Identity vs Role Confusion

Erikson suggested that the crisis facing people entering their teenage years is to learn to shape their own identity, or else face the perils of role confusion and aimlessness. This is often a confusing stage of life marked by experimentation as teenagers learn to find their own path, shaped by and often rebelling against social and parental expectations. From a developmental perspective, teenage paddlers who throw themselves wholeheartedly into canoeing, whether pursuing a serious competitive career or making a lifestyle choice to paddle full-time, are doing so to answer the existential questions of who am I and what can I be? They may be pulled in conflicting directions as they seek their answer. I've worked with young paddlers when they first join national training squads, often at the same time they are starting university or leaving home, when they are exposed to two very different social worlds. Their university and non-sporting friends are encouraging them to socialize, go to parties and have fun, while their canoeing coaches and teammates are encouraging the opposite, to work hard and remain disciplined. In pursuing a sporting identity, teenagers realise that they are called to make choices that can feel difficult, especially if they believe they will lose contact with friends who are following a different path. How an individual chooses to respond to these choices defines their identity, values and achievements in later life.

There are some beautiful examples of young paddlers taking this stage of life to the very limit, funding their kayaking adventures through filmmaking and writing. Here are a couple of quotes from some typical whitewater kayaking DVD covers:

*"...The story of a group of friends who have undertaken a journey to explore the limits of possibility...driven through the passions of nine of the sport's top athletes and lifelong colleagues, they experience a year of chasing their Dream Result."* [50]

*"Downunder the Horizon line follows 3 Australian kayakers on their trails around the globe, cameras in hand while working and hucking themselves overseas proving there is a way to live your dream without a dream bank account! It's a film about grabbing a boat and getting out there, the rivers of the world are waiting to be paddled!"* [51]

These productions are marked by themes of freedom, adventure, testing the limits, and fulfilling potential. There is a sense of optimism and energy that is inspiring, although when viewed from later stages of life they can also invoke regret at missed opportunities or frustration that the realities of life now make such adventures impossible to realise.

## Young adulthood: Intimacy vs Isolation

The next stage in Erikson's theory is young adulthood, taking place from the early twenties to late thirties. Erikson believed that the key challenge of young adulthood is to learn how to form and sustain a long-term relationship, which he framed as conflict between finding intimacy and emotional isolation from others. The attractions of an independent life, and perhaps a fear of painful rejection, can mean that some paddlers stay in a perpetual 'adolescence', living a free-spirited existence well into their middle years. Successfully starting a family and taking on the responsibilities of parenthood are society's typical expectations of this stage. I discussed the impact of parenthood in the previous chapter, and while it clearly doesn't necessarily mean the end of paddling, it has an impact on opportunity and motivation. In the right circumstances it's possible to keep competing as a parent, and there are powerful examples of paddlers who have combined parenthood with a long competitive career. Like slalom's Stepanka Hilgertova from the Czech Republic, still racing internationally well into her 40s.

AEphotos.co.uk / A Edmonds

The question of identity is often not fully resolved in early adulthood. Here are some moving words from Slovenian slalom paddler Ursa Kragelj, that capture the continuing search for individuality in early adulthood:

*"The improvement in paddling was good this year but the problem is I don't need improvement, I need a leap. Meaning a leap of thought, rather than a leap of technique, endurance etc. And because it will have to be a high jump without the pole (meaning: support), could even be a triple jump – I don't really care – I need to confront myself with my desires and fears. Because we can only be free when creative. And creativeness is the very core of our existence. Stop for a moment and listen to your voice within. In every single one of us lies a hidden treasure of creativeness, which craves to be expressed. The secret to find this treasure is to dare to be WHO YOU REALLY ARE. And when*

*you do, the ideas, thoughts, happiness and satisfaction starts pouring out like a volcano. It is that simple but why is it sometimes so hard?"[52]*

While it is possible to form and enjoy an identity as a full time athlete or paddler there are many reasons why this is not sustainable – the inevitable physical decline brought about by ageing, the financial cost of competing or travelling, the desire to broaden horizons or establish a 'proper' career, or the pull to settle down and start a family. Having invested so much in sport and achieving a robust sense of identity, the decision to stop racing or paddling at a high level is not always easy. As Campbell Walsh, Olympic slalom medallist, said of his impending retirement:

*"I've been living in a little canoe slalom bubble for most of my life, being lucky enough to pursue my childhood passion. To leave that, and enter the real world, actually have to work for a living, is a bit scary."[53]*

One factor to consider is the degree of success a paddler achieves and how satisfied they feel with their career. Consider Australian slalom paddler and Olympic medallist Kate Lawrence's decision to retire after failing to qualify for the London 2012 Olympics:

*"I can't help but grieve the loss of a future that I worked so hard for, but that did not eventuate. I am tired. I am emotionally exhausted. My dream is gone, and along with it the drive, the motivation, the spark that is necessary to enjoy and benefit from training 1, 2 or 3 times a day, 6 or 7 days a week for the foreseeable future."[54]*

Germany's Oliver Fix made a clear-cut decision to retire from competitive slalom after winning the 1995 World Champs and the 1996 Olympics. He said he had achieved what he wanted to and was ready to do something different – in his case travelling and studying in China before moving successfully into coaching. It's hard to call retirement as sharply as Oli did, and many paddlers go on a year or two beyond their best because it can be so hard to let go of one's sense of identity as an athlete. This speaks to a deeper question of self-esteem, and the journey everyone faces to grow truly 'comfortable in their own skin', confident in who they are, not just what they do. It feels special to be a member of a national team, to travel and compete internationally. Leaving this behind for a 'normal' life can feel like an anti-climax or in extreme cases, even bring a sense of failure. Perhaps this is one of the attractions that keep many ex-paddlers involved in the sport as coaches (or sport psychologists!). Yet I also know paddlers who retired and quite happily never looked at a boat again. I think that for these folks, competitive canoeing was more a means to an end rather than a passion in itself. Their motivation was to pursue goals and test themselves against the best – it just happened to be in a kayak.

Whatever the motivation to retire, it's important to be able to recognise and apply the insights and lessons from being a serious competitor to the rest of your life:

*"I do miss elite competition and sometimes find myself getting jealous of those who are still competing. Competition at any level teaches you so much but is a tough tutor. It is scary at any level and learning to control your fears and make the most of whatever talent you have is a great feeling. Sadly you are only ever a guest at the top end of sport, when your stay is over it is over and that is another lesson you have to learn."*

**Ivan Lawler, 6 time world marathon champion**[55]

**Middle adulthood: Generativity vs Stagnation**

Erikson believed that this stage of life is shaped by a desire to help others and make a difference by doing meaningful work. He coined the term 'generativity' to describe the concern of guiding the next generation through socially valued work, and helping others learn and achieve worthwhile results. Failure to do so leads to stagnation, the feeling of being stuck in a rut, living a meaningless life. This is the classic 'mid-life crisis'. Middle adulthood starts from the mid thirties or so, and might often be seen when paddlers move to coaching, instructing or volunteer roles in the sport. No longer prioritizing their own participation, many now get more satisfaction from enabling others to learn or improve.

AEphotos.co.uk / A Edmonds

But middle adulthood does not necessarily mean the end of active paddling – far from it. It's easier now than it has ever been for older paddlers to stay active, with improvements in equipment and a general trend in western societies for older people to remain healthier than in the past. Psychologically, people seem to settle on an 'inner age' that stays pretty stable – at least that's what I'm told by my active friends in their 70s, who claim they feel much younger on the inside. So in pursuing my second slalom career, I've been reminded of the growing difference between my younger self – stuck in my late 20s or in Erikson's terms somewhere between late adolescence and early adulthood, and the reality of being in my early 50s, and middle adulthood. At best, I reconnect with my competitive spirit, feel energised and challenged, and enjoy the buzz of paddling and racing. At worst, harsh reality hits when I see myself on video, or compare my running times with the top racers, and realise that I'm moving so much slower than I imagine!

Managing the gap requires constant attention, holding the dynamic tension between inner and outer identities. I think the trick is to fully 'own' the benefits that come with age rather than hanker after eternal youth. After all, maturity brings plenty of advantages in terms of broader experience, greater perspective and (perhaps) a more settled sense of self-confidence. Racing is no longer the most important thing that defines me, making it easier to compete without fear of consequences. At the same time, I enjoy tapping into my younger identity because it keeps me fresh and active. I hope I can continue to manage the gap through paddling, because it seems a relatively healthy way of dealing with the challenges of mid-life.

## Late adulthood: Ego Integrity vs Despair

From the age of 65 or so, the final developmental task is retrospection, ideally finding a sense of contentment and integrity from having lived a happy and productive life. A sense of despair is the alternative when the view back is on a life of disappointments and unachieved goals. By this age, it's likely that paddling will have become a more serene pursuit on lakes and sheltered water, although there were several slalom competitors over the age of 60 at the World Masters Games in 2013. For most of us this stage lies in the future, and is a reminder to make the most of the opportunities we have right now to get out on the water and stay active.

# Over to you

You might like to reflect on your own life and how you've navigated your key transitions – moving from education into employment, pursuing a career in sport or elsewhere, facing questions of retirement from competition, forming and sustaining a relationship, starting a family...what aspects of Erikson's life stages do you recognise from your own experience?

What role has canoeing played for you? Have there been times when it's been central to your sense of identity? Has it helped you by providing a haven away from life's other demands? What lessons have you learned on the water that can guide you in other aspects of your life?

47. The effects of age and exercise on short term maximal performance: A model based on physiological systems. Jim Martin PhD, Austin, Texas

48. http://www.acsm.org/docs/current-comments/exerciseandtheolderadult.pdf

49. http://en.wikipedia.org/wiki/Erikson%27s_stages_of_psychosocial_development

50. Dream Result, DVD by TEVA

51. Downunder the horizon line, DVD by Skippy films

52. http://en.ursakragelj.com/blog/stop-for-a-moment/

53. http://www.sportscene.tv/whitewater/canoe-slalom/news/campbell-walsh-one-of-britains-finest-canoe-slalom-athletes-retires

54. http://www.sportscene.tv/whitewater/canoe-slalom/news/farewell-from-a-fantastic-athlete-kate-lawrence

55. http://www.sportscene.tv/flatwater/marathon/news/legends-five-time-marathon-world-champion-ivan-lawler-reflects-on-his-fruit

# Chapter 11
## The experience of wilderness

In the three years between 1977 and 1979 I paddled several Tasmanian wilderness rivers for the first time. It was something of a pioneering golden age of canoeing, when it was still possible to make first descents and take multi day trips down remote rivers. Several river systems were threatened by hydroelectric development, and the fight to save the Franklin River became a major political issue in Australia.

One river system that didn't survive was the Pieman, which, along with its major tributaries the Murchison and Macintosh Rivers, is now a series of long narrow lakes on Tasmania's west coast, dammed as part of a hydroelectric scheme. I cried for the rivers' memory when I first drove over the new bridge that crosses Lake Murchison. The Pieman has a special place in my heart: in 1977 I paddled the river for the first time, a wide-eyed boy joining the Derwent Canoe Club's regular Easter trip. Only my friend Mouse was younger than me (he was 13 and I was 14) so it was a big step to paddle with the 'grown ups' – although the average age of the group was probably about 20. My kayak was a homemade fibreglass Lettman Olymp, which worryingly began to leak almost as soon as we set off. No one had proper dry-bags; instead we packed our gear in several plastic garbage bags inside a hessian sack. The 65 km trip took 3 days through remote gorges with Grade 1-3 whitewater, interspersed with long flat-water reaches.

Adventures began within an hour or two, when my friend Flan wrapped his boat around a log, snapping it in two. Luckily we were still close to civilization so he was able to climb out of the gorge and walk to Rosebery, a small mining town. I found the whole trip hard – my sleeping bag got wet so the nights were cold and uncomfortable, my boat leaked profusely despite my attempts at repairs, and my back ached from three long days of paddling.

Yet at the same time I absolutely loved the whole experience; camping on sandbanks or in rainforest glades amongst giant tree ferns, exploring tributary waterfalls, and running rapids with the added challenge of a laden boat and the knowledge that it was a long walk out if anything went wrong. All within the camaraderie and banter of the paddling group. Over the next few years I paddled the Pieman again along with several trips down the Franklin and a first descent of the Jane River in 1979. The Jane is a major tributary of the Franklin and is uncrossed by any roads. A friend drove us in along a 4WD track and then we dragged our boats the final 6 km to the river. We had no real idea what was in store, and made our way around siphons, through spectacular gorges and some extreme cliff edge portages. It took us three days to reach the Franklin, and another day and a half to reach civilization. The Jane has only been paddled a handful of times since then, after the access track was closed to protect the World Heritage values of the area.

# Going solo

Paddling alone in the wilderness adds another dimension that seems to intensify the whole experience. Here's how regular solo paddler Robin Scott describes his experience of a two-day trip on the remote south Ram in Canada:

*In addition to normal camping and safety equipment I had to take climbing equipment to portage two waterfalls. My boat was so heavy I did portages in relays. Between me and the nearest track were many miles of mountains and thick forest. In these circumstances any tiny mistake, such as the loss of a piece of equipment, could have serious consequences. This pressure gave me a concentration that I'd never felt before. I felt a strange reluctance to divert my gaze from the river downstream: I was completely focused on making forward progress, by whatever means. I didn't allow myself the luxury of enjoying the wild surroundings, or contemplating anything other than the immediate task in hand. In fact, although it was an intense and unique experience, in many ways I felt that I lost something by paddling alone, and that I had discovered a disadvantage of soloing[56].*

# Being outdoors

Even if paddling in the wilderness is not a regular option, there are many benefits from just being outdoors and on the water. Researchers now have evidence to back up what paddlers have known for years – that exercising outdoors is more beneficial for mental wellbeing than exercising indoors. Compared with exercising indoors, exercising in natural environments is associated with greater feelings of revitalization, increased energy and positive engagement, together with decreases in negative emotions like tension, confusion, anger and depression. People exercising outdoors also reported greater enjoyment and satisfaction and were more likely to repeat the activity.[57] These findings are underpinning the green gym movement, which encourages people to do productive work and exercise outdoors. Stress levels drop, and positive moods increase when people are active in natural environments like rivers, lakes or the sea. There are several explanations why this might occur.

Harvard biologist Edward O Wilson put forward his biophilia hypothesis – that humans have a deep-seated, ingrained affinity with animals and the natural world. This serves an evolutionary purpose because a love of nature, expressed through growing plants and keeping animals, has helped human survival over millennia[58]. Psychologists Rachel and Stephen Kaplan proposed that nature provides opportunities for effortless attention, like watching the clouds move across the sky, that allow a necessary restoration to the fatigue caused by directed, effortful attention, such as working on a computer. Roger Ulrich argued that nature aids recovery from all forms of stress, not just the fatigue of concentrating too much. He believes that seeing certain types of landscapes, those with open vistas and water, automatically triggers a positive emotional response[59]. In her research with adventure sport participants, including kayakers, Susan Houge Mackenzie and her colleagues found that being in a natural environment positively affected people's experience of flow states, when they became totally immersed in the task at hand, often losing track of time[60].

# The spiritual dimension

Being in a natural environment, especially if it's wild and remote, can trigger a feeling of transcendence – a deep sense of connection with nature, of being part of something greater than our individual selves. Many spiritual traditions have recognised the power of the wilderness and the need to retreat from the urgency of normal life. In early Christianity, the desert fathers and mothers lived secluded lives so they could pray and meditate in the wilderness. In Buddhism there is also a long tradition of monks and nuns leaving their homes and seeking freedom from their desires in the wilderness. From a Hindu perspective, God is ever present throughout every aspect of nature.

Whatever explanation you prefer, there is something special about being outdoors, and even more so to be active in truly wild places. I've been moved by these experiences from my first exposure to wilderness on mountaintops and in river gorges as a teenager, and as I get older such moments of transcendence feel increasingly important. I value more than ever the chance to be in a wild place and feel connected with a natural river. I might even call this a spiritual dimension to paddling. Carl Jung once said there are no problems of mid-life that don't have an underlying spiritual dimension. So in my mid-life, I feel fortunate indeed that kayaking still offers a basis for deeper experience and connection, a way of refreshing body and soul.

# Wilderness and the Fundamentals

**Mastery Motivation**

Wilderness environments often promote a sense of awe, of being connected to the wider world, in extreme cases leading to feelings of transcendence and a loss of personal identity. This can reduce feelings of competition with others, and create a more intense focus on self-mastery of immediate physical challenges. This contrasts with a typical competitive environment that usually reinforces individual identity.

**Execution**

Being in a dynamic, natural environment like a wild river seems to make it easier to experience peak states of 'flow' with heightened attention. This is because actions have more significant consequences and demand a higher level of concentration and commitment than less remote equivalents.

**Decision Making**

Remote environments bring added considerations when considering risk. An injury or broken equipment has greater ramifications when help is distant or exit from a river difficult. This typically leads to a more conservative approach.

**Teamwork**

Positive team relationships are even more important in wilderness environments and multi-day trips. Fortunately, the experience of paddling, camping, and negotiating a journey together can provide a strong foundation for trust and friendship.

## Questions to reflect on

What do you most appreciate and value about your own experience of wilderness and the outdoors?

Are you creating enough opportunities to feed your soul by getting outdoors and onto the water?

*Deb Pinniger*

---

56. *http://worldkayakblogs.com/robinsolos/ south ram 1 August 2013*

57. *http://science.naturalnews.com/2011/257053_Does_participating_in_physical_activity_in_outdoor_natural_environments_have.html*

58. *http://en.wikipedia.org/wiki/Biophilia_hypothesis*

59. *http://www.apa.org/monitor/apr01/greengood.aspx*

60. The multiphasic and dynamic nature of flow in adventure experiences. Susan Houge Mackenzie, Ken Hodge & Mike Boyes. Journal of Leisure Research, 45,2, 2013

# Conclusion

I set out in this book to answer some long-standing questions about the connection between what a paddler thinks and feels and how he or she performs. I hope that you have found something of value, whatever type of paddle-sport you enjoy as a direct participant, as a coach or the parent of a paddler. I love that this sport is so varied and offers so many different ways of having fun, overcoming challenges, and learning about life. Developing the four Fundamentals are essential if you want to be self-confident on the water and on the start line. They are also essential if you want to be successful anywhere else in life, so I hope you can use your experience as paddler to enjoy a happy and fulfilling life off the water, too.

Jonathan Males

# AE Photos

Antony Edmonds is a UK based freelance photographer. His sports portfolio covers a range of projects from local athletic events through to World and Olympic championships. These images can be found in UK and international news and sports publications and websites.

Antony has worked with a number of sports organisations to improve their image portfolio. For example, many of the images used here come from an ongoing collaboration with GB Canoeing to cover national and international regattas since 2008.

Antony can be contacted at:
antony@aephotos.co.uk

Lightning Source UK Ltd.
Milton Keynes UK
UKHW052312140419
340973UK00001B/4/P